THE ARTISAN WAY COLLECTION

Comprising the Dunlith Hill Writers Guides to Surviving the Writing Life, Professional Relationships, Sustainable Creativity, and Artisan Publishing

DEREN HANSEN

Dunlith Hill

CONTENTS

INTRODUCTION

Being a professional writer involves more than mastering the craft of writing and the art of storytelling. There are the constant challenges of managing your own expectations as a writer, dealing with other people in the industry, maintaining your creativity, and running what is, in truth, a small business.

This collection includes four Dunlith Hill Writing Guides:

Surviving the Writing Life: How to Write for Money without Going Crazy

Professional Relationships: How to Deal with the Characters you can't Re-write

Sustainable Creativity: How to Enjoy a Committed, Long-term Relationship with your Muse

Artisan Publishing: Why to Choose the Road Less Traveled

Together, they will help you explore an art-and-craft-centered approach to your writing life we call, The Artisan Way.

PART I.

_____

SURVIVING THE WRITING LIFE

_____

CHAPTER 1.

HARD QUESTIONS AND SOBER ANSWERS

You want to be a writer?

Ok, you're a writer.

While we exist in the physical world, we inhabit a **Matrix**-like universe filled with streams of encoded symbols. If we define writing as assembling strings of symbols in some medium—lists, notes, messages, letters, email, presentations, reports, and so on—almost everyone in the literate world writes. The fact that you have this book means you are thoroughly a part of the literate world, and thus are a writer.

"No," you say, "I want to *be* a writer."

Ah, you mean you want other people to call you a writer.

It is true that while almost all of us write, very few of us are called or call ourselves writers. That's because *writers* produce a particular kind of writing: work that is consumed by people in general instead of someone in particular.

Implicit in the dream of *being* a writer is the hope that you will derive some or all of your livelihood from your writing. That is, being a writer is usually synonymous with writing for money.

If you've ever entertained such a dream, this book is for you because it will help you explore two critical questions:

1. Why should perfect strangers trade their money for your words?
2. Are you willing to do what it takes to produce the kind of words strangers will want to buy?

WHY DO YOU WANT TO BE A WRITER?

People who say they want to write a book usually mean they want to publish a book. They take it as given that the book they produce will naturally have publishers bidding for the privilege of publishing it and readers lining up at the book stores to purchase it.

Why?

Because they wrote it: because they brought a prodigy into the world for which future generations will sing their praise.

Does that sound a bit over the top?

Think about it: does anyone set out to write a mediocre book? Does anyone dream of their book debuting to lackluster sales?

Publishing in the commercial market is a trying and exhausting undertaking. Yet I've met far more people who want to be published than want to release an album or play professional sports, even though the requirements for success in all three endeavors are similar. Like many things that take skill and dedication, writing at a professional level is not as easy as it looks.

So, why do lots of people believe they should be published?

- Many confuse a passion for reading with a need to write.

- A number think that because they can write they should write.

- Some want to prove they can write something better than the stuff that's out there.

- Some who can write fall prey to the *cute kid* syndrome and assume everyone will love their baby as much as they do.

- Others who say they dream of writing really dream of having written so they can bask in the glow of their accomplishment.

ON THE ULTIMATE GOAL OF PUBLICATION

Many would-be writers talk about the journey toward their ultimate goal of publication—as if writing is a sort of personal quest and publication is the Holy Grail. What's odd about this ultimate goal is that publication, in some form, is easier now than it ever was: if your quest is simply to publish, there are a variety of ways to achieve it that don't require agents and major New York publishing houses.

Of course, what we don't want to admit when we talk about our writing journey toward publication is that our goal is really vindication: we want the stamp of approval from the gatekeepers (agents, editors, and publishers) which will admit us into the ranks of the *published* authors and make us citizens of the shining literary city on the hill.

It is true that the personal experience of producing a novel is much like a journey. And it's perfectly understandable that we should want our largely solitary pursuits validated by other people. But the stark reality is that the publishing industry doesn't exist to bolster your self-esteem or even acknowledge your worth. The only thing that matters is whether you have a project that will appeal to an audience large enough to be profitable.

WHY SHOULD YOU PUBLISH?

With the advent of the Internet, there are more ways to share one's writing with others than ever before. You can publish anything you want, from the profound to the profane, in a multitude of formats—and many people already have.

Combine the exponential eruption of new material with the wholesale loading of everything that's ever been written onto the Internet and we have a situation where you wouldn't make a significant dent in the list of things to read even if you had a thousand lifetimes.

Why should you add a few drops to this rising ocean of information?

You might argue everyone has a right to express themselves.

Perhaps, but no one else has any obligation to pay any attention to that expression.

This brings us to the crux of the matter.

WRITING FOR MONEY ISN'T ABOUT YOU

If you intend to write for a general audience, the vast majority will neither know nor care about you and your reasons for writing. The only thing that matters to your readers, and the only reason they'll give you money for your words, is that your book gives them something—an experience or information—they can't get elsewhere or as conveniently.

If you understand this one fundamental truth about commercial writing, you'll be well ahead of the legions of would-be writers.

* * *

So what should be your motive for writing?

At one level there are as many answers as writers, but after you peel away motives like vanity and fame that can't endure the grueling course that is the life of writing, the only sustainable answer is that you write because you must.

Most people understand, "you write because you must," as a compulsion—which seems obvious when we're talking about the dedicated time and effort required to produce a hundred thousand words. But the compulsion to write is not a nameless force bubbling up from our subconscious. The answer we arrive at in the final chapter is that the reason to write is because you have something to contribute to the conversation.

In order to understand what that means and what you're getting yourself into, we will begin in chapter two with a look at the stamina, dedication, and self-confidence required if you want to write for a general audience. Chapters three and four explore the world of commercial publishing and your role in it as a writer. After an interlude in chapter five to help you understand how to make sense of the wealth of writing advice you're likely to encounter, we turn, in chapter six, to the mindset you'll need to develop to survive the writing life. In chapters seven and eight, we elaborate on the ways you can provide value to your reader when you understand your job as a writer and take a closer look at what constitutes good writing. Chapter nine concludes with a discussion of the ways in which you can contribute to the great conversation embodied in our written legacy.

None of this, of course, will guarantee you fame and fortune as an author—but then no book can (not even the ones that do). What it will do is give you the tools, in the form of concepts, expectations, and mindsets, to chart your own course through the seas of commercial publishing without going crazy.

CHAPTER 2.

NOT FOR THE FAINT OF HEART

Many writing books are like army recruiting posters: high on romance and adventure while glossing over the part where you wallow in mud, shivering through the blackest part of the night with a violent and gruesome death only a sneeze away.

The writing book equivalent of romance and adventure is motivation and encouragement. It's not that self-esteem, cheerleading, or inspiration for writers is bad—you'll need all of that to sustain you should you take up the burdens of the writing life—it's that it's inconsistent with a more sober discussion of what you need to be prepared to do if you want to be a writer.

If you say, "I want to be a firefighter," no one says, "You can do it, if you just believe in yourself and keep trying." Well, they might say that, but it will be a footnote to, "You'll have to get in condition so you can haul a hundred pounds of equipment up six flights of stairs while wearing a full complement of protective gear."

I'm certainly not saying writing is as serious an undertaking as firefighting. Nor should there be any confusion between a profession where lives are on the line and an endeavor that occasionally affects a life.

Nevertheless if you want strangers to give you money for your words it's going to take more than a can-do attitude and a boundless belief in yourself. The mental conditioning required to write and to persist at writing in the face of detractors, rejections, and indifference is similar to the physical conditioning required of firefighters. In both cases—though in very different ways and for very different reasons—you've got to be tough.

The writing life isn't an easy one. Most of us who respond to the call do so because of a deep drive or compulsion. And like the proverbial fools who rush in where wise men fear to tread, most of use embrace the writing life encumbered by fantasies, illusions, misconceptions, and outright self-delusion.

Having a clear picture of what you're getting yourself into won't necessarily make your writing life easier, but it will help you not make it any harder than it needs to be.

One of the most important things I learned as an anthropologist is that there are usually structural reasons for why things are the way they are. For example, half way through a steak we might laugh about the sacred cows of India, ignorant of the fact that on the sub-continent a living cow can feed far more people over time than one that has been turned into hamburger.

The publishing industry has a lot of sacred cows. If you understand the structural reasons behind the practices, your writing life will be much more peaceful than if you run around—because it's massively unfair, and slow, and so last century—shouting, "Where's the beef?"

Lest this sound too grim (and you're tempted to toss this book in favor of one that will tell you you're a special writer), there are things you can do to improve the quality of your writing life. In keeping with the Indian theme, most of them are about mind-set and have a Zen-like character—things that writers must simultaneously believe and not believe:

- You must care enough to pour your heart and soul into a book and not care at all when critics savage it, publishers reject it, and readers ignore it.

- You must believe your book to be unique and also know what other books it is like and how it fits into its genre.

- You must be your own best advocate and yet you must never believe you're so good you have nothing left to learn and are entitled to success.

- And perhaps most difficult of all, you must write only for yourself and at the same time you must write only for your readers.

Why do you write? Or, more to the point, why do you keep writing?

YOU WRITE BECAUSE YOU MUST

I write because I have a need, bordering on a compulsion, to get the story right.

I wrote parts of several bad novels during high school (along with stories and all the other things young people should try to write), but playing **Dungeons and Dragons** was the first real catalyst. A funny thing happened: I participated in a few games as a player, but it wasn't long before I found I was more interested in being the dungeon master. It was far more satisfying to set up the dungeon than to explore it. In fact, I noticed I was spending more time and getting more pleasure out of preparing the adventure than actually running the game. As the years passed, I noticed the same pattern as I produced music, software, and prose.

Like plants in the desert, your motivational roots need to run deep—usually down to the level of a basic compulsion—because the parching heat of the writing world will wither any motives with less staying power.

SOLITARY CONFINEMENT

Being a writer is a lot like being an iceberg: only ten percent of what you do is visible to others. It's not simply that you'll need to write a million words to produce the hundred-thousand word novel that is finally published; it's that you'll do ninety percent of that work by yourself.

Worse than working alone and unnoticed, your struggles will also be lonely ones because people who can truly empathize are few and far between. You'll spend most of your time:

- Staring at a blank page afraid that you've run out of words;

- Staring at a page full of words you wrote shocked that something so terrible didn't cause the universe to implode;

- Staring at your email desperate for some response to your query, proposal, or draft (and worrying that the rest of the world succumbed to the zombie apocalypse but no one bothered to tell you);

- Staring at the void in the mail box that should have been filled months ago by a royalty check;

- And staring at the long list of inferior writers who have waltzed past you to wealth and universal acclaim.

Overcoming your personal demons and developing the discipline to write and revise until you have something ready for public consumption is actually the easy part (because it's all under your control). Once you share your work with the world you'll need more stamina and a thicker skin than you thought was humanly possible.

SLINGS AND ARROWS

"Don't beat yourself up. The publishing industry will do it for you." – Julie Wright

If you don't believe in yourself, when it's time to publish your work, who will? If you're not your own best advocate, who's going to do it for you?

But there's more to this advice than a lets-feel-good-about-ourselves moment.

There's clearly a difference between self-criticism and beating oneself up. Where the latter is about grief spirals and pity parties, the former involves a realistic assessment of where you are and constructive plans to improve.

So, will the industry beat you up?

Yes, but not in the way you might expect.

There will, naturally, be people who hate your work and loath you—often for reasons entirely beyond your control. But the number of unambiguous foes, who would gladly beat you up if given the chance, is dwarfed by the vast majority of people who inadvertently beat you up because they need an excuse to not pay attention to you.

Think about it in terms of the query problem. An agent who gets thousands of queries a year when they might realistically be able to take on one or two new clients doesn't open each query hoping it will be a project they'll fall in love with. They're looking for the quickest way to determine if it's something they can safely ignore. It's nothing personal. It's simply the most rational way to deal with an avalanche of material.

The single most important way not to beat yourself up is to understand the true nature of the writing world. If you go in with false hopes and expectations you'll constantly be beating yourself up over things that are beyond your control.

And the single most important aspect of the writing world you must understand is rejection.

THE GREAT CHAIN OF REJECTION

If you follow all the advice from agents about query letters you will have invested days, even weeks in crafting your query letter, and hours researching an agent and personalizing your query for them. After all that work, a thanks-but-it's-not-right-for-me-good-luck, response (if you get any response at all) adds the insult that you were worth only about thirty seconds of the agent's time to the injury that they rejected your project.

What you need to understand, though it won't lessen the agony of the rejection, is that yours is only the first link in a great chain of rejection:

- agents reject authors
- editors reject agents
- publishers (or internal surrogates like the publishing committee or the sales team) reject editors
- booksellers reject publishers
- readers reject booksellers

Viewed in its entirety, it is a thing of beauty: your one small rejection is part of the great web of rejections that is publishing.

Put a little less flippantly, you need to understand that rejection doesn't mean much because everybody in the industry—writers, agents, editors, publishers—gets rejected by somebody else.

Unfortunately, acceptance doesn't mean that much either.

THE INSIDIOUS CIRCLE OF ACCEPTANCE

Clearly, having your writing accepted means that someone else thinks you've done something worthwhile. That kind of validation is undeniably powerful. And at a practical level, acceptance means a chance to get a return on the investment you made in your first project, and another turn at bat for your next project. But it doesn't mean that you've been magically transformed from a peasant scribbler into a princely author.

The Romans posted someone next to the conquering hero to whisper in his ear and remind him he was still a mortal, not a god, as they paraded past the adoring crowds. We need someone like that when acceptance and success come, particularly if they come too easily.

The fact of the matter is that acceptance is nearly as subjective as rejection. Consider, for example, how many bestsellers of yesteryear now lie forgotten on dusty library shelves and dark corners of used bookstores.

One of the downsides of publication is that the book is no longer entirely your own. Of course, you can't exercise the rights you've transferred to the publisher. But in a broader, practical sense, the more readers invest themselves in your books, the less freedom you have as an author (if you don't want to alienate your fans).

This isn't simply a game to find the positive in rejection and the negative in acceptance. The deeper, even-keeled truth is, rejection or acceptance, what really matters is that we keep writing, deliberately and consistently, unperturbed by the crests and troughs of the inevitable waves of the writing life.

CHAPTER 3.

THE WORLD OF COMMERCIAL PUBLISHING

It's comforting to believe there's something inherently noble about books; that pages covered with words and stitched together between covers represent a repository of compressed and distilled thought.

That's why the dissonance between books and the businesses that produce them is disconcerting—particularly the way in which content (i.e., your precious writing) often seems, at best, a secondary concern.

This chapter is about grounding your expectations. Unpleasant as it may be when you'd much rather indulge in literary fantasies, you need to understand the nature of the writing world in which you hope to make a home.

PUBLISHING IS A MARKET NOT A SYSTEM

Systems have rules which, if followed, produce consistent results.

It's both tempting and comforting to think of publishing as a system. As aspiring authors, we study examples of things that worked, from pitches and queries to hooks and books, driven by the faith that if we can just figure out the rules we too will be published.

There's only one problem: publishing isn't a system.

First, there's no governing body to agree upon and enforce the rules.

Second, it's not consistent. What works in one case may not work in others.

The publishing industry is like a high-security facility that would-be authors are trying to infiltrate. If an author manages to break in, everyone congratulates them and then the guards seal the breach, adding extra security measures to make sure no one else can ever get in that way again.

While that analogy may seem a bit cynical, the kernel of truth there is that it's different for everyone.

So, if publishing isn't a system, what is it?

"I know this one," you say. "Publishing is a business."

That's a better characterization, but it still falls short. *A business* implies organization, perhaps even a degree of centralization. The fact that the big publishers are all located in New York looks like centralization. But publishing is more than New York (sorry, Big Apple), and the many players, each pursing their own objectives, are not well enough organized to call them collectively, "a business."

The best way to understand publishing is as a market—not a commodities market (i.e., you can't replace writing with corn and have the same market), but a market just like the market for goods and services where you live.

While markets are clearly about things being traded, they're also about relationships among buyers and sellers. Why do you patronize certain stores and not others?

Probably because the people at the stores you prefer have done something for you, like remembering your name or giving you a discount.

In the context of a market, where customers can freely choose among vendors, following *the rules* doesn't guarantee that customers will buy from you. Will, for example, a restaurant that follows all the rules of good restaurants always succeed in a market where there are plenty of restaurants to choose from? No. The rules might be necessary for success, but they're not sufficient to ensure it.

If you want to participate in the market, you have to offer competitive goods or services. The rules of writing help define what it takes to produce a competitive novel. But once you're in the market, the game changes to one of relationships.

So stop wondering why no one has recognized the merit of your novel and get out, either figuratively or literally, and meet some people.

PUBLISHERS ARE RISK AGGREGATORS

Coming to publishing from a career in high-tech, it didn't take me long to notice the similarities between publishers and venture capitalists. Both, for example, take the lion's share of the equity and leave you with ten to fifteen percent of the business.

The similarity isn't accidental. Like venture capital, most media businesses—books, movies, music—are structured as risk aggregators.

"No," you say, "publishing is about culturally relevant ideas, experiences, and expressions. It's full of people who love books, not actuaries."

Perhaps, but staffing is a by-product of the economic logic of the business model.

Look at it this way: if you were presented with an opportunity to gamble on something that offered a massive payoff but required a substantial bet and had payoff odds of one in a hundred (i.e., you're going to loose your money ninety-nine times out of a hundred), and you could only afford to make the bet once, would you risk the money? No. But if you and ninety-nine of your closest friends pooled your resources—and the payoff was greater than the hundred bets you'd have to make—instead of squandering your money, the proposition becomes a sure thing.

Venture capitalists invest expecting seven out of the ten companies to fail, two to break even, and only one to succeed—where success means returning enough to cover the other bets and provide a profit. Publishers work in a similar fashion: most books don't earn out their advances, some (the mid-listers) provide a modest return, and a few produce stratospheric profits that cover the losses on all the other books as well as satisfying the shareholders' appetites (at least for a quarter or two).

One important but rarely mentioned implication is that as an author, part of what you're giving up when you sign a contract with a publisher that gives you an advance is the risk that even though you're good enough to get published your book might not sell well enough to provide a return on your effort. During the heyday of the advance system, which subsidized writers by decoupling compensation and sales, publishers in effect aggregated the risk individual authors took in writing their books—not because they were charitable but because developing talent reduced the publisher's risk over time.

So why are publishing companies structured as risk aggregators?

Because no one, absolutely no one, really knows what books will sell.

NOVELS AND NOVELTY

No one can predict how a particular book will do with any degree of certainty. There are many examples of books that came to the market with major backing and flopped and others no one in the industry paid any attention to until they left the bestsellers in the dust.

However, there is one thing the industry knows and relies on to sell: novelty.

We've been trained by our commercial culture to equate new with improved, or at least more important. Agent Janet Grant, holding forth on why we should resist the impulse to release trailers and book covers when they're created—which is often as much as a year before the book will be published—captured that spirit when she said:

> "... I soon start to think that the book is old news. Heavens, I've watched the trailer, I've seen the cover several times...didn't I read that book already? If I think I haven't read it, well, I just dismiss the book. I want to read what's new."[1]

It's no accident we call long-form works of fiction, "novels." The word comes from Latin, and means *new*—as in a new story (an important qualification at a time when high culture focused on retellings of Greek and Roman classics).

But *novel* is even more appropriate in a business whose engine is a relentless drive for novelty. This is partly because of the structural consequences of an industry where the product is 100% returnable, and partly because of the publisher's role as a risk aggregator. Together they create a constant pressure to produce big releases.

The industry's focus on the new is one of the fundamental ways in which the interests of authors and publishers diverge: authors, like soaring birds that can glide for hours on a single wing beat, strive for books that will produce a constant royalty stream for decades; publishers must beat their wings (with each release) to stay in the air because they need the constant boost of short-term revenue.

What's the take away?

Don't grudge other authors their moment in the spot light. Prepare for yours. Expect the moment to be brief. Then get busy on the next *new* thing.

PUBLISHING IS SLOW

With all the emphasis on novelty, you might assume that reducing the time to market would be good because it would allow one publisher to deliver more novelty than another. As with many other assumptions about publishing, that one is wrong.

Writing for publication is an exercise in extremely delayed gratification.

One of the things that makes self-publishing attractive, if your patience is anything less than saintly, is that with a traditional publisher the time between the moment you finish your book and the point at which it begins appearing on shelves in the book store is best measured in years.

Publishers acquire books roughly eighteen months before they will be published. Agents and editors can take months to read your manuscript before a contract is forthcoming. With all that, you could be looking at a two to three year interval between finishing a manuscript and seeing the book in a bookstore.

Why so long? Do publishers take some perverse delight in tormenting authors by stretching their dreams out on a temporal torture rack?

No. The excruciating time lags are merely structural. Large publishers have systems in place to make sure there are books in the pipeline to meet their future needs. The eighteen month publishing schedule includes time for editorial revisions, all the aspects of book production from cover art, layout, and design to buying paper and scheduling the print run, and about six months of marketing efforts prior to publication.

Agent Rachelle Gardner explains it this way:

"In reality, everyone is making decisions at exactly the speed they need to, in order to fill their lists. Sometimes it's slow, sometimes it's fast. But you can be sure that no matter where in the pile your project is, this process isn't all about you." [2]

It's hard to say exactly how the new world of electronic publishing will change publishing timelines, but one thing is certain: the time lags will never completely disappear. Editorial revisions will always take time. Electronic book production requires time to format files and test them on various readers. And it will still likely take six months of marketing effort after you publish to build an audience.

* * *

The one thing you must understand about the world of commercial publishing is that it all comes down to managing risk.

Publishers invest in editorial, production, and marketing efforts in order to decrease the risk that a book will not sell. The time lag between contract and publication reduces the risk that publishers won't have a full line of new books to offer each sales season. The relentless focus on novelty addresses the risk that demand for new books will slacken.

By the same token, the more convinced a publisher is that your project is a sure thing, the faster they'll move to bring it to market in order to reduce the risk that they'll make less money.

What does this mean for you?

With the exception of the risk that you won't deliver a contracted manuscript, commercial publishing is not about you because you're only one of the many risks publishers must manage.

CHAPTER 4.

YOUR ROLE AS A COMMERCIAL WRITER

Commercial publishing generates profits by distributing books to purchasers. You as the author are structurally incidental (even if you are a big part of the marketing effort) to the process after the publisher accepts your final manuscript.

If commercial publishing isn't about you, what then is your role?

WRITING IS THE BUSINESS OF PRODUCING AND LICENSING INTELLECTUAL PROPERTY

The fact of the matter is that anyone who wants to be a commercial author (i.e., someone who gets paid for their writing) is attempting to establish a business that produces and licenses intellectual property. The process by which you produce your intellectual property may feel like a journey, but your business partners (e.g., your agent and publisher) are only interested in your products.

I'm not saying that art and expression must take a back seat to business. Rather, with the possible exception of memoirs (and your support group), the people with whom you do business are only interested in you because of what's in it for them.

Think about it: when the traveling merchant comes to your village, do you ask them to tell you about their trip or do you ask them what they've got to sell?

THERE ARE NO WRITERS

With many occupations, you can say, "I'm a _____," because you earned some certification. Critical professions, where lives are on the line, require rigorous training and state-level licensing.

Not so with writers. Anyone can hang out a shingle and declare, "I am a writer." Perversely, there are few milestones that unambiguously identify one as a writer: even hitting the New York Times Bestsellers List only proves that you have written a popular book, not that you can do it again.

You're better off approaching the business as if there are no writers.

You might object that there are obviously a great many writers. Millions of books are published each year. Millions of people are employed in jobs where they produce words on paper (or screens). Beyond that, nearly every citizen of the literate world strings at least a few words into sentences each day.

All true. And yet most of this vast army of writers write in the service of some other purpose. Just as nearly every scientist uses mathematics to do their work but they don't call themselves mathematicians, the majority of people who write don't call themselves *writers*.

So what does it mean to be a writer?

In the world of commercial publishing, the only writers

who matter are the ones who have enough of a following that every book they release is a guaranteed bestseller.

In the world of the literati, the only writers who matter are the ones (usually dead) who have produced the masterworks of the canon.

It's pretty slim pickings if you're looking for a role model—which is the point.

Writers are like curry: it's an approach to preparing the food, not a particular dish. There is no single approved model of success or failure as a writer. Rather, like an entrepreneur, there's a world of opportunity and any number of creative ways to take advantage of those opportunities. Unlike other professions, where the pathway to achievement is clearly marked, writers have a blank page.

HOW TO HEAR SUCCESS STORIES

Aspiring writers are drawn to success stories, like moths to flames—and we're all guilty of a little twinge of jealousy that we aren't the subject of the story. But as inveterate optimists (what else can you call someone who devotes years to a single manuscript), we soak up the stories hoping we will one day be the hero of a similar story.

So it's deeply ironic that we who are storytellers often fall prey to the tricks of our own trade when we listen to these stories and then afflict ourselves with unrealistic expectations. We hear, for example, of a writer who went from query to book deal in thirty-seven days, note that our own queries have gone unanswered for more than thirty-seven days, and conclude that we're not worthy.

Why do we, of all people, do this?

Because we forget that the foundation of the

storyteller's art is to skip the boring bits. Advice about pacing, pithy dialog, and scenes (like, "in late, out early") all comes down to artfully avoiding the boring stuff that is an inevitable part of real life.

And if the tables were turned, how would you tell your success story?

Fresh from the process of scrupulously scrubbing all the boring bits out of your manuscript would you say, "Then on the following Tuesday, I wrote 1673 words. But when I looked over the new material on Wednesday, I decided I needed to rework half of it so I didn't reach my new word count goal that day ..."

No, you'd apply your craft and weave together a concise narrative of the highs and lows of the experience with a sprinkling of lessons learned. Above all, you would make it a story with protagonists, antagonists, try/fail cycles, a climax, and a denouement.

Why?

Because that's the essence of what we, as storytellers, do.

The next time you hear a success story, remind yourself that it is a story. Learn what you can from it, but don't compare it to your experience because you simply don't know all the boring bits that were skipped to make it a good story.

ON AUTHORS' PARTICULAR SUSCEPTIBILITY TO HOOKS

Perhaps it all started when Dr. Seuss rhymed about a nook with a book on a hook—his secret marketing advice to writers—though it's more likely hooks have been doing extra duty as symbols and metaphors ever since that day long ago when a proto-fisherman noticed an oddly shaped bone and said, "I wonder ..."

As writers, our literary livelihood ultimately depends on how often we're read. In order to catch as many readers as possible, reel them in, and leave them in the bottom of the boat gasping for more story, we use a wide variety of hooks.

If you've had more than passing exposure to the community of commercial writers, the first thing that comes to mind when we say, "hook," is either a pirate captain or a pithy one-liner, carefully designed to compel you to read more. Story hooks often take the form of an improbable juxtaposition (like, "I always hated warthogs until the day I turned into one,") that force the reader to wonder how such a thing could be.

There are many other kinds of hooks: covers, tag lines, jacket copy, author blurbs, reviews, book trailers, bookmarks, and so on. In fact, a good story is filled with hooks, large and small, that pull the reader deeper into the narrative.

Hooks are all well and good for readers, but they pose a subtle yet real danger to writers: we hear a hook, imagine the story we would write, and then get jealous because someone else has already written it.

Except they haven't.

They've written the story they imagined when they heard the hook, not the one you imagined. Like the blind men and the elephant, give ten writers the same hook and you'll get ten different stories.

It's part of the more general grass-is-greener phenomenon. We look at the success of others and imagine how their assets would solve our problems, being completely unaware of the problems they have that their assets can't solve (e.g., they may be rich but in poor health), or what it may have cost them to acquire those assets.

So appreciate and use hooks for what they are: ways to draw readers into your story. And remember, writers, as you try not to be jealous of either a book or its hooks, that a hook is only as good as the book it pulls you into.

WRITER ZEN: FAIRNESS AND YOUR MONKEY BRAIN

One of the ideas I gleaned from studying a biography of the Buddha is the Zen notion of the monkey brain.

The first image of a monkey brain that springs to mind is likely that of a frenzied simian bouncing around the cage of desires in which Buddhists would say we are trapped. But I found another, intriguing association with the phrase, "monkey brain," in a study that showed brown capuchin monkeys have a strong sense of fairness. The monkeys were trained to trade researchers pebbles for food, usually pieces of cucumber but sometimes grapes. If pairs of monkeys made the trade and one of them got a better deal (i.e., more grapes), the other would throw a fit. [3]

Does this sound familiar?

What if I replace *monkey* with *writer* and *researcher* with *publisher*?

More familiar now?

The fact of the matter is that the business of publishing is grossly unfair. Someone will always get a bigger advance, or more marketing support, or better reviews for their inferior work. Some young person will toss off a novel in their spare time to national acclaim while your decades of dedication to honing your craft will go completely unnoticed.

Your options are to embrace your monkey brain, throw a fit, and go sulk in the far corner of your cage, or to transcend your monkey brain—particularly the part that keeps oh-so-careful track of how fair the situation is—and keep writing.

CHAPTER 5.

WRITING ADVICE

Like other worlds in the social universe, the writing world is full of factions and camps. While it is true that everybody faces essentially the same struggle when it comes down to putting words on a page, the reasons they have for doing so and the criteria by which they judge whether the words are good differ. If you're just starting out, you're going to hear a lot of advice and that advice will be full of contradictions and inconsistencies. What follows won't wrap everything up and tie it with a bow, but just as understanding the nature of publishing as a business helps you adjust your expectations, understanding the diversity of writers and writing communities will help you make sense of their advice.

KINDS OF WRITERS AND THEIR ADVICE

One of the implications of quantum mechanics, which has provided fodder for many a writer of speculative fiction, is the notion that there are universes in which every possibility is played out because the root universe branches into two new ones at every decision point.

Whether the real universe behaves this way or not, the writing universe has split several times, and is in the process of doing so again.

If we don't count business writing and academic writing (about subjects other than writing), there are three writing universes for fiction: professional, commercial, and the new, uncharted reaches of the electronic frontier.

PROFESSIONAL

The word *professional* comes from, *profession*, which comes in turn from, *profess*. The modern sense of both *profession* and *professional* is entangled with notions of highly-trained—and highly-paid—specialists. With all those dollar signs dancing in our eyes, we lose sight of the root verb, "to profess," which means to espouse a body of knowledge and practice, and is also associated with the old, clerical notion of a calling.

The universe of professional writing fills the far-flung universities and MFA programs, where, in what is essentially an academic patronage system, publishing is simply a step on the way to the real goal of tenure as a writing professor.

Many writers aspire to be professional in the modern, highly-paid sense of the term, but go about their task more in the old sense of something to profess: literature is a calling, complete with commandments and a canon.

COMMERCIAL

Commercial, of course, comes from, *commerce*. The commercial writer is all about business: What are the trends? Where's the market? What are editors buying?

The universe of commercial writing orbits New York City. (A cynic might say New York is the black hole at the center of that universe.) This universe is all about advances and royalties and what's new. Commercial writers like to say that unpublished writers talk about books, published authors talk about money.

ELECTRONIC FRONTIERS

There was a time when the distinction between professional and commercial came down to labels like *literary* and *genre*. Writers in both universes had to squeeze through the same funnel because the only way to reach a large audience was through the distribution system controlled by the publishers.

We're now entering a new universe (or perhaps a hyperspace) of writing in the inter-webs where it's possible to publish your message to the world in a growing number of ways with the push of a button. Compared to the others, with their fairly well defined paths of advancement, this strange new universe is a wild west where there's one gold rush after another.

The problem with gold rushes, in case you slept through American history, is that by the time you hear about them the fist-sized nuggets have all been picked up.

ADVICE

I've painted with a broad brush to characterize the universes of fiction writing. In doing so, I've surely missed a host of important details and qualifications. But this brief illustration is sufficient to show that the path to success in each one is different.

What that means, in practical terms, is that when

someone gives you writing advice you need to take the universe they inhabit—and the one you inhabit—into account. It's not that the advice is mutually exclusive—or that a writer can't exist in multiple universes—but that each context has different priorities. For example, a commercial rule like, "dive right into the action of the story," may not be as important in a professional story.

It's easy to see the writing world as a monoculture. But you'll be happier—and do a better job of finding adaptive strategies—if you think instead of a multiverse teaming with variations.

BUT THEY BROKE THE RULES

How often have you heard writers complain that a best-selling author tells a good story but is a terrible writer? How about critiques that someone writes beautiful prose but the story doesn't go anywhere?

If we peel away the petty jealousy for those who collect royalties when we collect rejections, the allegation that someone broke *the rules* and still succeeded often comes down to writers in different universes complaining about each other.

Annette Lyons characterized the two great camps of writers as storytellers and word smiths. At one level, storytelling vs. word-smithing simply echoes the distinction between commercial and literary fiction, where the former is all about the story and the latter is about how the story is told. [4]

At a deeper level, storytelling and word smithing represent two fundamental approaches to the way we share narrative information. Storytelling is about selecting and presenting the most interesting bits. Word smithing is about telling a bit well enough that it's interesting in its own right.

So, does this mean we have to choose sides?

No, the two great values of understanding the nature of the different writing universes—and the species which inhabit them—are peace of mind and wisdom. You can enjoy greater equanimity when you realize you don't have to join any camp. And you're free to increase in wisdom by applying the best advice from each universe.

For example, instead of worrying about who broke the rules and got away with it from the perspective of a storyteller thesis or word-smith antithesis, apply the synthesis and strive for a good story, well told.

WRITER ZEN: FORESTS AND TREES

So, how should you deal with contradictory advice?

For example, in a comment about what matters in a query, agent Holly Root said:

> "Write the best book you can, then the best query you can. Submit written materials to agents. The worst they can say is no so don't worry about fine-tuning that to the nanometer ..." [5]

In other words, don't worry too much about the details.

Nathan Bransford (when he was still an agent) chimed in on the same topic and said:

> "I was thinking I'd discuss how if you ... act in good faith and send the best query you can you're going to be fine and there's no need to sweat the tiny details. [But] it is about the details in the sense that we are actually making a decision

based on a short letter and maybe some sample pages and so of course it's about the details." [6]

So, it is about the details.

How do you worry about the details without worrying about the details?

One thing that sets us apart as novelists is our ability to see the big picture. We may agonize over a word or phrase, but we should never lose sight of the role of those words in the scene, and the role of the scene in the chapter, and so on. It is our ability to see both the trees and the forest of which they are a part that enables us to tell the larger story.

Similarly, we need to see the bigger picture when it comes to advice about writing, the business of writing, and the writing universes. The difference between a pro and a wannabe is that pros don't lose sight of the forest and obsess about a single tree.

CHAPTER 6.

SURVIVING THE WRITING LIFE

Surviving the writing life depends on your day-to-day expectations. Just as you'll be happier in a relationship if you can accept your partner as he or she is instead of wishing you could change them, you'll be a happier writer if you understand and embrace the realities of the writing life.

JOURNEYS AND DESTINATIONS

It is fashionable among scribblers and would-be scribblers to talk about their writing journey.

At first I thought it a nice metaphor for the Zen of traveling well, the value of stopping to smell the proverbial roses, and the importance of enjoying the process over the product. It's also a concise (and gentle way) to help aspiring writers understand that the endeavor upon which they've embarked is likely to take a long time. But metaphors are at least a two (and sometimes three) edged sword. The edge on this one that might hurt you, if you're not careful, is that a journey implies a destination.

The problem with publishing is that there's no destination. There are certainly milestones, but in this industry the journey never ends: breaking in doesn't mean you've arrived, it only means you're a player; publishing a bestseller doesn't mean you're set for life, it only means you get another turn.

Part of the problem is simply structural: in the market that is commercial publishing, like Hollywood, regardless of what you did yesterday, the only thing that matters is, "What have you done for me today?"

"Wait," you may protest, "when people talk about their writing journey, they mean their personal development as a writer."

Perhaps. But can one ever reach a point where they have completed their personal development as a writer? Are there authors who have mastered their craft and truly have nothing left to learn?

Now I'm not arguing that you don't measure up as a writer if you're not constantly producing new material. Quite the opposite: you should write because you want to write—because you've got something to say—not because it's required for the journey.

My critique is more fundamental: the very notion of a writing journey does more harm than good because it encourages aspiring writers to look forward to the day when they reach their destination. In other words, it's the writer's equivalent of saying, "I'll be happy when I _____ (win the lottery; get a better job; lose some weight; etc.)"

It's wiser and more satisfying to live, and learn, and love in the present.

Write your current project so that if you write nothing else you can still say proudly, at the final accounting, "I am a writer."

And if you must have a travel-related metaphor, writing is like being a nomad in the desert: it's not about getting to any place in particular; it's about living well where ever you are each day.

REASONS TO STOP WRITING

One of the secret fears that haunt would-be writers in the wee hours of the morning, when sleep is scarce and we have no choice but to peer into the existential abyss, is the question, "Will anything come of my writing, or am I wasting my time?"

The good news is that this fear is both natural and common to our species. In fact, it's necessary: we'd never bother to revise and improve if we didn't have the slightest doubt about the perfection of our prose.

The bad news is that sometimes the answer to that fearful question is, "Yes."

As Chuck Wendig put it:

"Writing is a career that offers a tireless parade of moments emblazoned with self-doubt and uncertainty where you're forced to ever reevaluate who you are and why you do this. You'll often have to hold up your dream and examine it in the harsh light of day just to see how substantial it really is."
[7]

So how do you know if you'd be better off doing something else?

Some of the signs Wendig discusses are:

- *"You'd much rather talk about writing than do actual writing."*
- *"You spend your time doing everything but putting words on paper."*
- *"Your production levels are* [nonexistent]*."*
- *"That teetering tower of rejections threatens to crush you and your cats."*
- *"You think writing is about something (like working from home or being rich and famous) besides writing."*
- *"Writing is an endless Sisyphean misery."*

My aim in highlighting Wendig's signs isn't to depress you, but to make the point that until you're under contract you have no obligation to write. Specifically, you have no obligation to write novel length manuscripts and attempt to sell them to traditional publishers or release them electronically for people to buy.

We live in a time when there's almost no limit on the ways in which you can express yourself. From blogs to videos (with a detour through flash mobs somewhere in the middle), the opportunities to sound your barbaric yawp over the roof tops of the world are multitudinous. [8] (Ignore, for the moment, the fact that a multitude is simultaneously yawping.) Perhaps there are other media that are a better fit for your particular genius.

And if you return from the abyss with your dream intact, then it's a substantial dream and worth pursuing.

CARING AND NOT CARING

You've looked into the darkness and you're still sure you

want to live the writing life, so what's the first thing you need?

A thick skin.

As writers, we must both care and not care in order to succeed.

- You've got to write what you love—giving the story everything you've got—and then not get even mildly perturbed by all the rejections it garners ("It's not personal, it's just business") as you proceed to pour heart and soul into the next project.

- In public—say, for example, at a signing—you must treat everyone as your friend and yet you mustn't pay any attention to reviews (positive or negative) from your erstwhile friends or take umbrage that none of them have actually bought your book.

- Authors, agents, editors, and other publishing professionals are (at least in public) our colleagues and we must never grudge anyone for getting their inferior work published, or the fact that ours languishes for lack of marketing dollars, or bring up the glaring lack of editorial oversight, or ...

It's easy to become cynical, behind our cheery public facade about the consensual illusion we call the publishing industry, if we aren't careful to chart a course that preserves our integrity. (And by integrity I mean wholeness, not simply honesty.)

In other words, we must care enough, but not too much:

- We must take care to do our best work but not invest so much of ourselves that our self-esteem rises or falls with our work's fortunes.

- We must take care to be grateful for the people who take an interest in our work but never fall into the trap of believing we're entitled to their attention.

- We must be courteous and kind to all the people with whom we brush shoulders on a professional basis without paying too much attention to their successes or failures.

When it's all said and done, we need the quiet confidence to proceed cheerfully down our own path.

THE ZEN OF TAKING IT PERSONALLY

With all the frustrations endemic to publishing, we generally do well to remember that it is a business and, whatever happens, we shouldn't take it personally. The form rejection your query received doesn't mean you're a bad person who should never be allowed to put pen to paper again. It only means that the agent wasn't compelled—for any number of reasons, many completely beyond your control—by your query.

But as with many things in the world that are more nuanced than black and white, there is another level at which you should take it personally. Agent Howard Yoon said:

"Take everything personally. If you get rejected, take it personally. Do better. Find out ways to improve yourself so that you don't get rejected again.... Don't blame the industry or the market or the system. Take it upon yourself to improve YOUR chances." [9]

"But," you may ask, "isn't that completely contradictory?"

"How can you both take rejection personally and not take it personally?"

Ah, herein we find another Zen riddle.

You must not take it personally in any debilitating sense: don't allow a rejection to make you question your worth as a writer—or a person. Don't let the agonizing lack of response deflate your dream.

At the same time, you must take it personally in a constructive sense. Don't comfort yourself with the thought that a rejection is evidence of an agent's lack of vision. Instead, take responsibility for the fact that your query didn't work and ask what you can do to make it better, or to do a better job of finding agents who are likely to be interested. Or perhaps your story isn't as compelling as it could be (or another might be more compelling). In the end, the only thing that matters—and the only aspect of the process over which you have control—is the question, "What can I do?"

EXCELLENCE AND ELITISM

In your quest to do all you can do, you need to be aware of the fine line between excellence and elitism.

A hundred or so pages into a middle-grade fantasy I ran into a sentence that began, "Suddenly he slowly ..." I stopped short, wondering how the editor let that oxymoron get by.

Then I paused. Aside from that construct (which was

one of no more than five debatable craft points I'd noticed), the book was really quite good. So what had the editor done? They had likely caught the dozen, or hundred, or thousand other things that I never saw because those issues were resolved before the book was released.

In a note about finding critique partners who can give you meaningful feedback, the author said something to the effect of, "So I wouldn't give my manuscript to someone who liked [a wildly popular book, riddled—according to many in the on-line writing community—with craft flaws]." My first reaction was, "Of course not. I'd want someone with more refined taste." Upon reflection I realized that if I want to reach the largest possible audience, I should try to understand how and why something that might have had a few less-than-perfect elements managed to strike a popular chord.

It's easy, when you're trying to follow every rule, to think less of another work that shows what you see as evidence of less care. It's particularly tempting to do so when that other work achieves greater success than your own. And there's false comfort in justifying your work by blaming the unwashed masses, who wouldn't know quality if you hit them on the head with it. But the truth of the matter is that the masses, washed or not, are irrelevant where excellence is concerned. Excellence means striving to do your very best. It does not mean dismissing everything with flaws.

WHICH IS THE HIGHEST WRITING VIRTUE, PERSISTENCE OR PATIENCE?

Sometimes the answer—perhaps the most difficult

answer—to the what-can-you-do question is, "Stay the course and be patient."

When we're talking about the process of writing, particularly writing in the long form, persistence is clearly the most important virtue. If we expand our scope to the writing life, patience trumps persistence.

You might argue patience and persistence are both aspects of devotion—that both imply sticking with something even if you don't want to.

That's true, but there's an important distinction between the two virtues: persistence implies something more active than patience.

Here's what writer Natalie Whipple said about having a book on submission:

> "What I was least prepared for was the loss of control. It was easy to have faith in my agent, but at the same time it was strange not being able to do anything. I just have to…wait. In querying, when you get a rejection you can send another letter out.… I was so used to working for myself, and now my writing fate is out of my hands." [10]

For those of us who cope with difficult situations by finding something constructive to do, cases where the only thing you can do is wait are extremely trying.

The wannabe-writer-sphere is so full of encouragement to keep writing that it leaves you ill-prepared for the time when the writing is done and the waiting begins.

"But isn't that when you should work on your next book?"

Yes, of course. But for some of us it can be very difficult

to accept the fact that there comes a time when there is nothing more we can do to improve the chances of success for the book that's on submission—that there's no more scope for persistence—and that patience is the only way to continue.

PATIENCE AND READERS

Patience with yourself is only one of the many kinds of patience you need as a writer.

The work of writing itself is a patient undertaking. It's hard to maintain an average output of more than a few thousand words per day. And when you factor in revisions, it's not surprising that many writers produce only one novel a year.

There are a host of other ways in which a writer must be patient: Critique partners need time to read; like Rome, an online presence isn't built in a day; and promotion takes constant effort.

I thought I understood and was prepared for all of the dimensions of writerly patience, but there was one I didn't anticipate: I underestimated the degree to which writers must be patient with readers. You see, as an author, you're always going to be ahead of your readers because you're working on the next book while they're enjoying the one that was just released. That means you can't talk about the cool stuff on which you're presently at work and which occupies most of your attention. Instead you must try to match your reader's enthusiasm for something you thought was all kinds of awesome last year without succumbing to the temptation to spoil their fun and say, "Yeah, but that's nothing compared to what's coming!"

FINDING BALANCE

When you embark upon the writing life, you need to be prepared to be in it for the long haul. There are other endeavors where enthusiasm and industry will carry you through to success. Writing and publishing are slow enough that the only way to succeed is to outlast detractors and distractions. It all comes down to sustainability.

Have you ever tried hopping instead of walking? It doesn't take long before you get tired, and yet we can walk all day. The reason is that walking is about balance and a gait that allows our muscles short rest and recovery cycles between exertions.

A balanced writing life is similar: it is as important to allow our writing muscle to rest and recover as it is to exercise it every day. Like the afterburners that give a jet fighter a burst of speed but burn up fuel at a far higher rate, you may need an occasional push to get something finished on time, but it's not something you can keep up for long without crashing and burning. If you want to be able to stay in the writing game, you've got to avoid the trap of too much of a good thing.

You will, of course, have to find your own balance—everyone's natural gait is slightly different. But there are some general principles of sustainability that flow from the foundational wisdom of moderation: identify the things that are important to you and structure your days so that you can attend to all of them.

What's interesting is that when you stay on top of things, the amount of time they require each day is relatively small. To cite a simple example, if you rinse a dish and put it in the dishwasher after you've used it you'll never have to face a soul-crushing mountain of dirty dishes.

Beyond simply coping, you need to spend time on the things that make your life meaningful.

SOURCE OF INSPIRATION

The word *inspire* comes from a Latin root that means *to breathe into*. Many creation stories, for example, begin with the creator breathing life into his or her creation.

What breathes life into your writing, your work, and your very existence? What fills you with joy in being? Whatever it may be, take time each day to reconnect with the source of your inspiration.

IMPORTANT RELATIONSHIPS

For good or ill, humans are social animals. Much of our sense of who we are is a function of those with whom we are close. Put another way, much of what we do is motivated by the people with whom we have the most important relationships. Some have pursued their art at the expense of those relationships and wound up with the prize but no one to share it.

Take time each day to acknowledge and nurture your important relationships. Not only will you have more support right now, you'll likely have someone who appreciates it when you succeed.

HEALTH AND WELFARE

As Count Rugen says, in **The Princess Bride**, "If you haven't got your health, you haven't got anything."

If you neglect your basic physiological needs, you will reach a point where those needs prevent you from writing. Take time each day to care for yourself: get enough sleep, exercise, and eat well.

WRITING

Take time each day to write. If you are serious about writing it should have a high priority. While writing every day is an important habit, if you can't manage that you should still do something related to writing each day to keep in touch with your passion.

SOMETHING PERSONAL

There's magic in having a room of one's own. Having a project of your own makes it easier to compromise when you're working on someone else's project. Taking time each day to do something only you care about is essential if you don't want to lose track of yourself amid all the demands placed upon you.

MACRO BALANCE FLOWS NATURALLY FROM MICRO BALANCE

Like the performer who can keep a set of spinning plates balanced on sticks, taking time each day to connect with the five most important things in your life will go a long way to helping you find balance.

And don't think of it as balancing your life. The job of balancing an entire life is overwhelming. But keeping your days balanced is doable. Like writing a novel: you'll fail if you sit down to knock out 60,000 words, but you'll succeed if you write a thousand words a day for sixty days.

WE ARE OUR OWN PROTAGONISTS

As the protagonist approaches the climax of your novel, you pull out all the stops, throw everything at them, and turn what was a difficult situation into an impossible one. It's a good thing real life isn't like that—except sometimes it is.

Writing a novel is like the journey of the hero in our stories. We undertake the project confident we're up to the task of embodying our vision in words. There are setbacks along the way. And at least once during the project there comes a time that things look dark and the prospect of finishing seems impossibly remote. Like Frodo marching across the plains of Mordor, the end is plainly in sight yet it feels as though we'll never get there.

The analogy is particularly strong when we have only a few chapters left to write: we know exactly where they're going and they're chock full of exciting stuff, but Heaven and Hell seem to conspire to use up our every waking moment to keep us from finishing.

If we're half as good as our protagonists, we'll recognize those situations as the time for renewed resolve. And we may console ourselves with the thought that the degree of opposition must be a sign that we're producing something really good. But what it really comes down to—what sets us apart as novelists—is that, like our protagonists, we doggedly push through to the end.

CHAPTER 7.

YOUR JOB AS A WRITER

The astute among you will have noticed I just called you writers even though I argued a few chapters ago that there's no such thing.

Another Zen riddle?

No, in this case the apparent contradiction comes from the difference between internal and external expectations. There are no writers in the sense that there are doctors, lawyers, and other licensed professionals: aside, perhaps, from becoming a tenured writing professor there are no established and accepted career paths that will, if followed, make you a nationally-acclaimed novelist. The only common denominator among the handful of people we recognize as writers is that they wrote a lot for a long time. Schooling, jobs, writing habits— everything else is incidental from a predictive perspective.

And yet there is a time when it is important to call yourself a writer.

CALLING OURSELVES WRITERS

Sarah Callender said:

"I don't know about you, but for a long time, whenever a well-intentioned someone asked what I did professionally ... [i]t just felt so audacious, not to mention goofy, to utter the sentence, "I'm a writer!" ... We writers need to see ourselves as writers so that others will see us as writers.

"But ... we writers need to do the very, very hard work that will give us the knowledge, the certainty, that even if we are still unpublished ... we are writers because we put our tush in the chair and get words on the page every day." [11]

Allowing yourself to be what you're preparing for but have not yet achieved is what we mean when we say, "fake it till you make it."

By calling yourself a writer, you have both the permission and the obligation to make a dedicated effort. If you're serious, for example, about keeping a job, you'll do what's necessary to get yourself out of bed, make yourself presentable, and arrive at work on time—and you'll do it every day of the work week. When other demands or distractions arise, you say, "I'm sorry, but I have to go to work."

Similarly, calling yourself a writer means adopting the discipline of a writer. Discipline is more than simply writing each day (though that's certainly a good start). You need to focus not just on doing the job each day but on getting better at the job each day.

Thinking of writing as your job may seem like a sure-fire way to leach all the joy out of it, but if you treat it as an indulgence you'll either feel guilty or succumb when another good thing comes along to occupy your writing time.

The key point is that calling yourself a writer means you accept the hard work that comes with the title. *Writer* isn't an entitlement; it's something you live up to.

WRITERS WRITE

Nathan Bransford provided ten commandments for happy writers. His last three summarize your job as a writer:

> "8. **Park your jealousy at the door**. Writing can turn ordinary people into raving lunatics when they start to believe that another author's success is undeserved. Do not begrudge other writers their success. They've earned it. Even if they suck.
>
> "9. **Be thankful for what you have**. If you have the time to write you're doing pretty well. There are millions of starving people around the world, and they're not writing because they're starving. If you're writing: you're doing just fine. Appreciate it.
>
> "10. **Keep writing**. Didn't find an agent? Keep writing. Book didn't sell? Keep writing. Book sold? Keep writing. OMG an asteroid is going to crash into Earth and enshroud the planet in ten feet of ash? Keep writing. People will need something to read in the resulting permanent winter." [12]

If you take only one thing away from this book it should be this: the job of a writer is to write.

But your job isn't simply to put words on the page any more than a musician's job is to produce a stream of random notes from their instrument. What sets a musician apart from a student who can make not altogether unpleasant noises is the control and precision with which they play.

THE RESPONSIBLE WRITER

Some people describe writing in terms of a dream-like state and argue that it's a purely artistic, right-brain endeavor. I find writing requires both brains: while I'm envisioning a scene with my left brain, I'm searching for the best words with my right. Whatever the division of labor among the hemispheres, writing is a conscious act. And it is, therefore, something for which you as the author are responsible.

You are responsible for your words. There is no excuse for lazy, imprecise writing, including clichés, excess adverbs, or thoughtless constructions. In conversation you can say, "It's like, you know …" and if your listeners nod, they probably do know what you mean. But you have no such luxury with the written word.

You are responsible for the way you string your words together. To the reader your words should feel as effortless and natural as an intimate conversation. Yet, like a master mason who places each brick so that it is both perfectly aligned with its row and also does its part to make the wall strong, you must use words that both fill their grammatical roles and at the same time contribute to the larger goals of the paragraph and the piece.

Your job as a writer is to master language and the modes and techniques of expression that most clearly convey your thoughts. At a practical level, this means responsible writers constantly ask themselves, "Is that the best I can do?"

MEANINGFUL CONTEXTS

Your responsibility as a writer extends beyond the words that make up the book because your job is to produce a whole that is greater than the sum of the parts. You do so by creating meaningful contexts.

Researchers once arranged for a virtuoso violinist—someone who regularly played to packed halls of avid music lovers, who had gladly paid hundreds of dollars for their tickers—to play for commuters in the subway. Out of the throngs, only a few, most of them children, paused for beauty.

It's easy to hear that story as an indictment of the desensitizing elements of modern life. But there's a deeper structural issue: the virtuoso was out of context. The music coming from his violin was no different than it would have been on stage, but it had to compete with the noise and confusion and perverse acoustics of the subway. Nor can we know how many commuters recognized the virtuoso or wanted to appreciate the music but could not stop because they had business or commitments elsewhere.

Context helps us determine why we care.

As authors, we create macro and micro contexts.

Micro-contexts are what we call, "good writing." They include all the internal details—beginning with the well-crafted first sentence and running all the way to the satisfying conclusion—that collectively give us reasons to care about the characters and their story.

Macro-contexts are like the service and presentation at a fine restaurant. They frame and give emphasis to the work. While marketing and promotion are part of the macro-context, it is a broader notion that encompasses all the things that help us decide why we should care about the book.

WHAT ABOUT WRITER'S BLOCK?

Writing is like a muscle. If left unused, the muscle atrophies until you're unable to use it. The basic strategy of physical therapy is to move the muscle, forcing it to relearn its range of motion. It's a painful process because you're constantly pressing up against the limits created by your injury.

In a similar fashion, if you've had a writing injury, you need to keep putting words together until it no longer hurts to do so. Confronting the pain is an essential part of getting past writer's block.

There's only one sure-fire cure for writer's block: write.

I like to work on back-stories. If that doesn't do the trick, I'll write something totally unrelated.

You also need to understand that the real block is fear: fear you'll write something wrong, or it won't be up to par with your previous efforts, or no one will like it, or it doesn't come close to the pictures in your head, or … The list of fears, as you can easily imagine, goes on forever.

Fear is debilitating unless you can set it aside—not ignore it or wish it away, but set it aside. You do so by acknowledging your fears and then moving on.

The best way to overcome fear in writing is to plunge ahead, carried forward by the faith that at some point you'll look back on the trail of words in your wake and realize they're not all terrible—in fact they're better than you feared.

CHAPTER 8.

GOOD WRITING

As a musician, I have a problem. It's my own fault, really—and it goes all the way back to those childhood practice sessions I either skipped or muddled through until I'd done my time. You see, when I play, what the poor folks forced to listen hear is nothing like the music I think I'm playing.

It's like the illusion that the moon on the horizon is much bigger than the same moon riding high in the sky. You might swear that it really does look bigger on the horizon, but if you take a picture of the moon in each position (taking care, of course, to keep the camera settings the same) and measure its size, you won't see any difference.

Fortunately, there's help for people with my musical affliction. It's called audio software. With a composition package I can set down the notes and refine them until what comes out of the synthesizer matches the music in my head. While this doesn't guarantee that another person will have the same emotional reaction to the music, it does guarantee that my lack of technical proficiency no longer creates a gap between what I intend and what they actually hear.

We have a similar but more subtle problem as writers. In this day, when the vast majority of writing passes through computers, the legibility of our writing is rarely a problem. We take it for granted that most people will see the same words we put down on the page. If they see the same words, they should understand the same things when they read those words, right?

Unfortunately, it's not so simple.

WHY OUR WRITING IS BETTER THAN OTHER PEOPLE'S

Meaning arises from interpreting the words and the ideas you associate with those words. What may seem like a perfectly innocent statement to one person could have offensive connotations for another. We say reading is subjective—that readers bring their own baggage to the story—without appreciating how deeply true it is. If you really think about it, it's a miracle we understand each other as well as we do.

All of which is why we think (though most of us are too polite to say it) that our writing is better than most other people's: we know what our words mean when we put them down. With another person's writing, we only have their words and have to add in our interpretations and associations to produce meaning.

One of the reasons you might call other people's writing bad is if you can make no sense or get nothing meaningful out of it. It doesn't matter what they intended the words to convey. It only matters what you get out of them. This is why, no matter how certain you are of your writing's perfection, you need editorial feedback—you need to hear how other people react to your words.

The music in your head may be astonishing and sublime, but no one will ever know it if they can't hear the same notes.

NO ONE IS PUBLISHING GOOD BOOKS ANYMORE

Claiming your book will stand out from the rest because no one publishes good books any more is one of the first things agents mention when asked to list elements of queries that mark you as an amateur. I have a twinge of guilt each time I read a list like that because, try as I might, I can't exorcise the opinion that my book is actually better than most others. Now before you rush to get your torches and pitch forks, let me explain the epiphany I had as to why this heretical opinion is both true and false.

TRUE

As a writer, you must believe your book will be better than most comparable books. If you believe others are producing better books than you ever could, why torture yourself trying to write when you could simply sit back and enjoy their work?

"Wait," you say, rising up in righteous indignation born from proper writerly humility, "there are masters whose inkwell I'm not worthy to refill."

The problem here is the word *better*, because it implies a single comparative dimension when in reality novels can be good in many different ways. The *better* you have to believe in as a writer is that you have something to add to the conversation in terms of both the story you want to tell and the unique way in which you can tell it.

FALSE

But, as a writer, you also have to understand that you are writing for an audience—a paying audience—and their opinions and tastes are all that matters when it's time for money to change hands.

So, how do you know what your audience wants?

Short of conducting your own interviews and surveys, the best thing to do is forget about *good* and *bad* and pay attention to the books people are actually buying.

Which brings us full circle: the problem with claiming your book will stand out is that you're saying you know better than the market and everyone involved with it.

TRUCE

What can you do to keep your head from exploding?

Believe in your secret heart that your book will be better as you write. And if you've mastered showing instead of telling, your readers will discover for themselves how right you are.

GOOD AND BAD WRITING

I've long been puzzled by declarations that a commercial author is a *good* writer or a *bad* (but usually quite successful) writer. Clearly there are people who haven't mastered the basics of written communication and whose writing, because it is unintelligible or fails to communicate, we would all agree is bad. But if a piece has gone through an editorial process before being released for public consumption, presumably most of the basic mistakes have been corrected. So when we say an author is *good* or *bad* we must be talking about something other than their ability to put together coherent sentences, paragraphs, and scenes.

Of the few network television sitcoms I've enjoyed, nearly every one stayed on the air for one or two seasons too many. In some cases the final season was so disappointing that it soured the entire series for me. It was a rare series that delivered consistently and came to a graceful and satisfactory ending.

In sports, the players generally considered to be great are the ones who were consistent performers.

Do you see the pattern?

What we're really doing when we pronounce some author good or bad is stating an opinion of their ability to consistently deliver good stories with satisfying conclusions.

Assuming you want to be a good writer, you must understand that mastering the craft is necessary but not sufficient. Nor will an occasional burst of brilliance do. The patience and balance we've discussed provide the essential foundation for consistent storytelling and satisfying conclusions.

BREAKING THE RULES

While discussing comma splices (i.e., independent clauses joined by a comma, creating a run-on sentence) in her manifesto for correct punctuation and grammar, **Eats, Shoots & Leaves**, Lynne Truss, said:

> "… so many highly respected writers observe the splice comma that a rather unfair rule emerges on this one: only do it if you're famous…. Done knowingly by an established writer, the comma splice is effective, poetic, dashing. Done equally knowingly by people who are not published writers,

it can look weak or presumptuous. Done ignorantly by ignorant people, it is awful." [13]

One of the rules we throw at would-be writers is that they mustn't be bound by convention and shouldn't be afraid to break the rules. Unfortunately, this well-intentioned advice leads many writers to get ahead of themselves by trying to break rules they don't understand.

There are countless examples of authors where one is lauded while the other condemned for making the same writing, "mistake." As arbitrary and unfair as that may seem, it's simply a matter of demonstrated mastery: if you've shown your readers you know what you're doing, they'll try to understand your intent in breaking the rules; if you haven't, they'll take it as evidence you don't know what you're doing.

CHAPTER 9.

THE GREAT CONVERSATION

The **Great Books** series from the University of Chicago was published on the belief that the classics are part of a great conversation spanning thousands of years. While the vast majority of our current literature probably doesn't qualify for such exalted company, it is part of the great collective conversation we're having now.

The single most important aspect of your job as a writer is to have something to say. You may have mastered the technique of creating beautiful sentences, but that beauty won't hold readers if your words have no substance. But it's not enough to say just anything. The harder and more specific question you must answer is, "Do I have anything to say that will contribute to the conversation?"

Like other existential questions, it's not one you can easily answer. A quick, "Yes!" or, "No," is as likely to be wrong as it is right because you can't know until you try. You see, we all have a great deal to say, but outside of our circle of relationships, very little of it is worth anyone else's time. (Look at the vast majority of what flows through social media systems each day.)

Collecting and expressing your thoughts in a way that will entertain and enlighten total strangers is not easy. The question is as much about your stamina as it is about the originality of your thoughts.

It's also about your willingness to understand what has already been said before you start spouting off. Are you prepared to do the work necessary to follow the conversation so that when you offer something it's a contribution, not an interruption?

WRITE WHAT YOU KNOW

Doubtless you've heard the advice to, "Write what you know." It's at least as old as L. M. Montgomery's **Anne of Green Gables**, in which the precocious red-head publishes a story about Avonlea after her high-minded romances have been rejected.

"But," you object, "we wouldn't have hobbits and Narnia if we only wrote what we know."

That would be true, if you took the advice literally.

Like the gossip game, where players relay whispered messages and then laugh at the garbled version that comes out of the end of the chain, we've received only a degenerate version of the advice.

We should say, "Write what you know, not what you think you know."

L. M. Montgomery's Anne thought she knew the style in which she should write. Contemporary writers often think they should write in a particular genre or to a particular audience because they think they know what's hot.

Distinguishing between what you know and what you

think you know is often difficult because most of what we know is actually what we think we know.

Perhaps it would be less confusing to say that writing what you know isn't about the facts and information at your command, or even about your experiences. Writing what you know is fundamentally about what you understand.

The advice to write what you know should also be understood as advice to, "Write what you love." Sometimes your heart knows what you know better than your head.

That's why, if you love a world no one else has seen yet, you can honestly say you're writing what you know.

UNIQUE IN CONTEXT

The very act of writing implies (even if the ultimate product is derivative) that we believe we have something new to say, something to add to the conversation, or something that hasn't been said in quite the way we want to say it.

And yet, when it comes time to promote the work, everyone from agents and editors to readers wants to know what it's like so they can place it in context. The classic Hollywood log-line, where we say *new movie* is like *movie one* meets *movie two*, is an extreme, but concise way of putting a new project in context. The same is true for the genre, audience, and comparable books we're supposed to include in our query letters.

The frustrated author might ask, "How can my work be both unique and at the same time like something else?"

The enlightened answer to this Zen riddle arises from understanding that uniqueness is relative and only measurable in context. Uniqueness, in terms of novelty not rarity, is best understood as a measure of the degree to which the new work exceeds or changes the expectations defined by the context in which the work is experienced. The original Star Wars movie (episode four for you youngsters), was unique when it premiered because its design and special effects gave it an almost documentary feel compared to contemporary space operas.

The deeper problem with claiming uniqueness in your query is the implication that this entitles you to instant market recognition. It's the literary equivalent of walking into a cocktail party and shouting, "Everybody shut up and listen to me."

Your job is to add something relatively unique to the conversation. But before you can add, you must be a part of the conversation and understand the context. In concrete terms, this means you must read more than you write.

ADD SOMETHING TO THE CONVERSATION

But take care that the pendulum doesn't swing too far in the opposite direction. Loving a genre and wanting to read more of a particular kind of story isn't enough, in and of itself, to justify writing a book—nor is wanting to publish so that you can join the cool kids who have books with their names on them.

There is no shortage of underwhelming books. It's not that they are bad, but that they followed well-trodden paths and feel like more of the same. That's why we need to take care that we're producing something new instead of a *me-too*. There's nothing wrong with loving a book and wanting to do something like it, but before you take the trouble to draft an entire novel, ask yourself whether you have something to add to the conversation.

So how can you be sure you're adding something?

Many of the people who give advice about writing are quick to say that nothing kills a story faster than having a message. A corollary is that if you have a message, you shouldn't write fiction.

There is a real danger of allowing something about which you feel strongly to subvert your story, but if you don't have anything to say your story is, at best, nothing more than a *me-too* exercise.

So what's the difference between a message (bad) and something to say (good)?

It's the difference between a conclusion you want to promote and an idea you want to explore.

It's the difference between a lecture and a conversation. Readers have no patience for the former but they're happy (sometimes eager) to engage in the latter.

As an added benefit, the words will come more easily when you have something you want to talk about— ideas to explore, scenarios to play with, and possibilities to consider. Your job is to explore the conceptual landscape and invite the readers to play with the ideas they can uncover along the way.

CHAPTER 10.

CODA

Why do we write?

Is it because we need to be heard—because we have something to say, ideas to share, and emotions to express?

Perhaps.

But why do we read?

There are writers of such celebrity that people do, truly, want to hear what they have to say simply because they say it.

That's not me, and I'm willing to bet it's not you.

We read because we want to get something—a mix of information, emotion, and experience—from the work.

The most important lesson you can learn as an aspiring writer is that the reader is the only one who matters in this relationship. Stop worrying about expressing yourself as a writer and focus on delivering compelling experiences to your readers.

As part of your new-found focus on readers, you also need to worry less about getting published. Part of the reason, of course, is that the major houses in New York are no longer the only way to reach readers. But beyond that, getting published doesn't guarantee success. Consider this variation on an old philosophical question: if a tree is cut from the forest, pulped into the paper on which your book is printed, and sits on the shelf until it is remaindered, is it any different from a tree that falls in the forest with no one to hear?

"What makes you an author?
"Readers.
"It doesn't matter if you're published. Being published is nothing. It is everything to be read."
— Tracy Hickman

There was a time when the fact that you'd labored with pen or typewriter long enough to produce a manuscript meant something. Unlike mere mortals, authors had the super power to fill a ream of paper with words. Now any idiot can copy and paste multiple books a day.

More to the point, a great many people who are not idiots have invested the time and effort to produce interesting and worthwhile books. Readers will no longer read your words simply because you put them together and they have nothing better to do.

If you get nothing else out of this book, you should take away one great secret: even though you're the only one who can write your books, when it's all said and done it's not about you.

PART II.

_____

PROFESSIONAL RELATIONSHIPS

_____

CHAPTER 11.

IT'S NOT ABOUT YOU

When asked where they get their ideas, writers often say they listen to the voices in their heads. Perhaps it's because they want readers to experience their characters as vivid and self-willed. And yet the rarely acknowledged fact of the matter is that those characters can always be rewritten.

Unfortunately that's not true for characters that exist outside your head. Other people—real people—have an annoying tendency to go off-script and you have no option but to take them as they are.

While you can't correct people with a flourish of your pen, the good news is there are time-honored—and time-tested—ways of interacting with other people to create and build relationships that even writers can master.

OLD SCHOOL NETWORKING AND SOCIAL MEDIA

Dale Carnegie's **How to Win Friends and Influence People** was originally published in 1936. How could an advice book published before World War II still be relevant?

Publishing, like nearly everything else in our lives, is fundamentally about human relationships. And people haven't changed much over the last century. If you brush aside the cobwebs and blow away the dust, you'll find Carnegie's 1940s-era advice is as good as or better than the latest pearls of wisdom from social networking gurus.

And what does Carnegie advise?

Here's a summary of the principles of **How to Win Friends and Influence People**:

FUNDAMENTAL TECHNIQUES IN HANDLING PEOPLE

- Don't criticize, condemn, or complain.
- Give honest and sincere appreciation.
- Arouse in the other person an eager want.

SIX WAYS TO MAKE PEOPLE LIKE YOU

- Become genuinely interested in other people.
- Smile.
- Remember that a man's Name is to him the sweetest and most important sound in any language.
- Be a good listener. Encourage others to talk about themselves.
- Talk in the terms of the other man's interest.
- Make the other person feel important and do it sincerely.

TWELVE WAYS TO WIN PEOPLE TO YOUR WAY OF THINKING

- Avoid arguments.
- Show respect for the other person's opinions. Never tell someone they are wrong.
- If you're wrong, admit it quickly and emphatically.
- Begin in a friendly way.
- Start with questions the other person will answer yes to.
- Let the other person do the talking.
- Let the other person feel the idea is his/hers.
- Try honestly to see things from the other person's point of view.
- Sympathize with the other person.
- Appeal to noble motives.
- Dramatize your ideas.
- Throw down a challenge and don't talk negative when the person is absent, talk about only positive. [1]

How does this apply to writers?

The key to winning friends and influencing people, in both the art and business of writing, is empathy. You can't capture characters or readers without it.

Empathy is no more or less complicated than putting the other person first.

The single most important take away from **Surviving the Writing Life**, the first of the **Dunlith Hill Writing Guides**, is that it's not about you: the vast majority of the people with whom you'll do business as a writer—particularly your readers—care about a relationship with you only because of what's in it for them.

This volume takes that theme and, using Carnegie's principles as a framework, explores the ways in which you can navigate the variety of professional relationships you're likely to have as a writer.

We begin with a careful look at Carnegie's three fundamental techniques in handling people and how those techniques provide the foundation for your professional relationships as a writer. Chapters two through four explore, respectively, "Don't Criticize, Condemn, or Complain," "Give Honest and Sincere Appreciation," and "Arouse in the Other Person an Eager Want." Chapter five applies some of those insights to the challenge of approaching and working with agents. In chapter six, we consider Carnegie's, "Six Ways to Make People Like You," and then look at particular applications of those principles as you find and build your audience in chapter seven. Chapter eight reviews Carnegie's, "Twelve Ways to Win People to Your Way of Thinking," which we apply in chapter nine's introduction of a principled approach to marketing and promotion and chapter ten's look at author platforms.

In the world before pervasive interconnectivity, getting published was the writer's Holy Grail because the publisher, who controlled the book distribution system, was the key to getting into bookstores and ultimately finding readers. Now writers have additional ways to reach readers. And, more importantly, readers now have ways to find and acquire books that don't include bookstores.

Tracy Hickman summarized the new reality for writers:

1. *"What makes you an author? Readers."*
2. *"The challenge now is to find your audience, not your publisher."*
3. *"The future of publishing is to find, connect with, and maintain your audience."*

The way in which you establish a professional relationship with your readers makes all the difference. And the key is to remember: it's not about you the author; it's about what you, the author, can do for your readers.

CHAPTER 12.

DON'T CRITICIZE, CONDEMN, OR COMPLAIN

The simplest way to improve people's estimation of you is to stop being mean. Dale Carnegie gives examples of employers who saw a measurable increase in productivity and morale after they stopped shouting at their employees.

For writers, who interact with other people via the written word as much or more than they interact fact-to-face, this principle means you must discard any sense of entitlement.

Yes, you've written a book.

It's a non-trivial accomplishment.

But the fact that you've written something doesn't obligate anyone else to read it. You are not entitled to the attention of agents, publication, or commercial success. Once you accept that fact, you'll find you have much less to criticize, condemn, or complain about.

What about all the things outside of your control?

Like students who gripe about the cafeteria food they eat every day, it's satisfying, even soothing, to belly-ache about the publishing industry: to criticize the author who effortlessly churned out a sub-par book that's flying off the shelves; to condemn publishers who throw seven-figure advances at pointless celebrity books; to complain about the arcane query processes that blind agents to our masterpieces.

But stop and think for a moment: while it may feel good to rail against the publishing industry, just as it may feel good to chew out a slacking employee, these are the very people you want on your side. Wouldn't it be better to have employees at whom you never need to shout? Wouldn't it be better if the people in publishing wanted to work with you because you understand—at least to some degree—what they're going through?

COMMERCE AND CULTURE

Complaints, criticisms, and condemnations sometimes arise from misunderstandings or serve to mask ignorance. Much of what literary types grouse about comes from forgetting the difference between commerce and culture: we like to think that books are about culture, but we have them because of commerce.

It would be nice if the industry, particularly publishers and book stores, were committed to providing readers a variety of culturally relevant voices, but thanks to the ghost of Adam Smith and his invisible hand, it won't happen. You see, market driven economies are very good at oversupplying a perceived need. That's why, for example, three different (and all terrible) *Lambada, the Forbidden Dance* movies were released within weeks of each other in the mid '90s. The moment something seems to be gaining popularity authors, publishers, and book sellers rush to that part of the cultural spectrum in the name of being responsive to readers (and shareholder's) needs.

And every one of those commercial players is complicit in creating a kind of cultural imperative that shouts, "This is more important than other stuff, everyone else wants it, and you should too."

Once you accept that the market for the written word, by its very nature, is fickle and most definitely not fair, you'll be less inclined to complain. Instead of condemning the industry and wishing it were different you'll find ways to spend your efforts on something constructive—improving those things over which you have control and those relationships where you can have a positive influence.

Understanding the nature of the market and the endeavor of writing for money is the first step toward a professional approach to writing.

BEING PROFESSIONAL

Do you know what it means to be a professional writer?

- You know that professional writers work hard at writing, often revising one book, drafting another, and outlining a third all at the same time.

- You know that professional writers work constantly at promotion in every venue, both real and virtual, they can find.

You know it's a lot of work, but you believe you're up to the job. You're willing to put in the time and effort. But have you considered what you'll have to give up?

One of the things you must give up as a professional writer is your private opinions. It's not that you can't have opinions; it's simply that you're no longer at liberty to share indiscriminately.

Why?

Because professionals must work with everyone.

A relation, who works for the State Department, explained that prior to being sworn in as Foreign Service officers they were told they had to give up partisan politics because it would be their job to represent the entire nation when posted to the various embassies. Of course they would still vote, but their participation in the political process would have to be a private matter as long as they were in the Foreign Service.

As a professional, you don't have the luxury of alienating people, particularly in an industry as small as publishing where there's a real chance you might have to work with them at some point in the future. Tracy Hickman said, "There's only one thing you can be sure of: you never know who you're talking to, so treat everybody as important."

More generally, being a professional means it's not about you, it's about what you can do for someone else.

The mantra of the professional is:

I am a professional.
I don't have problems.
I don't cause problems.
I solve your problems.

When you need a doctor, the last thing you want to hear is that they're having a bad day: how they feel—so long as they are able to do a competent job—is irrelevant when you need medical attention. Similarly, when someone reads one of your pieces, the only thing that matters to them is whether you can inform and entertain.

A professional approach to writing means that even if your complaints, criticisms, and condemnations are perfectly justified you simply don't go there.

So how can you overcome your natural tendency to grumble?

The best writing advice I ever received was something whose importance I didn't truly appreciate until long after I'd forgotten who gave me the advice. This is what they said:

KEEP YOUR EYES ON YOUR OWN TEST

Jonathan Lethem discussed the same notion in terms of golf:

> "You're not playing against the other people on the course. You're playing against yourself. ….. The reason Tiger Woods has that eerie calm, the reason he drives everyone insane, is his implacable sense that his game has nothing to do with the others on the course. The others all talk about what Tiger is up to. Tiger only says, I had a pretty good day, I did what I wanted to do. Or, I could have a better day tomorrow. He never misunderstands. The game is against yourself. ….. Just you and the course." [2]

I attended a writing conference as a presenter. One of the guests was a prominent author with whom I hoped to make an acquaintance. Aside from attending one of his panels, I never ran into the author during the conference—which wasn't a surprise: he's a busy man.

But as with the Tango, where it takes two, part of the reason I missed the author is because I was busy, too.

During one of the battles of the Civil War, a subordinate rode up to General Grant, gave his report, and then asked if the general was worried about what the confederate general might do. "No," replied General Grant, "I'm worried about what I'm going to do."

The single biggest temptation to criticize, condemn, or complain comes when we compare ourselves with others. Like golf, it doesn't matter what anyone else does: you're the only one who can write your book. Complaining about the sweet deal another writer got won't help you finish your manuscript.

Beyond the improved productivity you should enjoy by focusing on your work, the positive way in which you go about creating new material will go a long way toward attracting readers and supporters.

CHAPTER 13.

GIVE HONEST AND SINCERE APPRECIATION

Have you considered how fortunate you are?

First, those of us who write (or attempt to write) are afforded a privilege denied to a substantial portion of the world's population: we have food, shelter, opportunity, and a sufficiently stimulating environment that collectively give us the ability to write and something interesting to write about.

Second, we have people around us who support our writing.

Third, in a world where a million other things compete for everyone's attention, there are people who take their time to read what we write. No one is obligated to read our words. That someone chooses to do so is a gift.

Even in the ultimately self-interested world of commercial publishing, the time and attention of a professional is something to be appreciated. A form rejection doesn't tell you much, but compared to indifference it at least gives you some information about the people who may not respond to your work.

HONEST APPRECIATION

Appreciation, however, goes beyond merely acknowledging those from whose efforts we benefit directly. Honest appreciation is a willingness to recognize and acknowledge good without reference to how it may affect you.

It is, in fact, this element of disinterest that makes giving honest and sincere appreciation such a powerful technique for building relationships. We all have an arsenal of defenses to counter people who approach with requests. We are powerless, however, to resist a sincere compliment.

As simple as it sounds, giving honest appreciation is a surprisingly difficult thing to do well. Most of us are handicapped because we're congenitally self-centered. And if we manage to get beyond ourselves, we often trip over the one thing that qualifies our compliments to be honest appreciation: they must be sincere.

How can you become more honest and sincere in your appreciation?

HONESTY THROUGH EMPATHY

One of the best ways to develop an appreciation of something is to try doing it yourself. You'll often discover that there's a lot more to something that looks easy to a casual observer.

No one who wants to be a musician believes they can do so without practice whereas many aspiring authors believe they can simply sit down and bang out the great American novel. Perhaps the problem stems from the fact that we call the endeavor writing. Viewed as the act of putting words together, writing is something most of us do on a daily basis. Couple that experience with nearly constant reading—our environment is replete with words and symbols—and it's not nearly so illogical for people to think they can write.

Once, however, you sit down to show all those people publishing mediocre novels how it's really done and start putting words on the page you discover a hidden world of complexity, anxiety, and frustration. If nothing else, your attempts to write should give you an honest appreciation for the incredible amount of work and dedication required to produce long-form writing.

SINCERITY THROUGH PARITY

There's a subtle and often overlooked aspect of giving honest and sincere appreciation: no matter how sincere the appreciation you express may be, if the social distance between you and the person to whom you express the appreciation is too great it rapidly loses sincerity. Thanking a virtuoso for a moving performance is appropriate, fawning about their technique smacks of sycophancy: the more you protest, the more the person on the receiving end wonders about your ulterior motives.

In terms of social calculus, the most sincere appreciation comes from peers.

This brings us to networking—yet another thing we're supposed to be doing to build our careers. The value of well-placed relationships seems clear in theory, but how do you put theory into practice?

Doug Eboch said:

"What Joe was trying to do I would call "networking up."

In other words, he's trying to build a relationship with someone more successful than he is. That is a logical way to go but actually not the most useful kind of networking. Tom Cruise networks with Steven Spielberg, I don't. I don't have much to offer Spielberg and real networking is a two way street." [3]

Thinking about Eboch's advice I realized most networking success stories I've heard focus on networking up: making that critical connection to someone who can give you a break. Perhaps that's because, though rare, that kind of narrative makes a better story than, "I made friends and we did stuff together for years before finally making it."

The networks that pay real dividends day-in and day-out are formed among peers who sincerely appreciate each other because they have something to offer each other.

So how do you do it?

THE BEST NETWORKING ADVICE EVER

Eboch offered the following suggestions:

- **Nobody is doing you a favor.** *"If you are talented and your work is good, you have value in the business relationship."*

- **It's an ongoing relationship.** *"When you meet someone the goal should be to build that relationship not to get them to do something for you."*

- **Nobody is unimportant.** *"The guy delivering your script could be a major player long before your movie ever gets* made." Corollary: *"What you need to be looking for is talent and drive."*

- **Quality is the commodity.** *"All the charm in the world will not help if you don't deliver good work."*

- **Don't put your energy into trying to impress someone who's much further along than you are.** (Chances are they don't have the time or energy to pull you up to their level anyway.) Instead, look to peers—people in roughly the same place as you—and see if there might be some place where two heads are better than one. [4]

* * *

If, after all of this, you're still not convinced that giving honest and sincere appreciation is the right thing to do simply as a matter of principle, then consider this: all other things being equal, agents, editors, and even publishers will choose to do business with the author who comes across as pleasant and personable (because, believe it or not, those publishing industry professionals are human too). Giving honest and sincere appreciation is one of the most effective ways to be the author with whom they'll want to do business.

CHAPTER 14.

AROUSE IN THE OTHER PERSON AN EAGER WANT

Dale Carnegie spends a fair portion of the first section in his book hammering home the point that other people couldn't care less about what you want. Uppermost in their minds is what they want.

What does this have to do with writing?

According to Carnegie, the best way to get someone to do what you want is to show them that it is in line with something they want. For example, he shares a letter a freight company sent its customers detailing all the problems they had when customers delivered goods late in the afternoon and then suggests a better letter would concentrate on the benefits (e.g., no delays) that customers who could arrange to deliver their goods earlier in the day would enjoy.

What do we want when we query?

To secure representation or publication.

What does the agent want?

A project they can sell without too much effort.

Because there's no way to know what will sell, the best

way we can give a prospective agent what they want is to write a compelling book, make sure our project is a good fit, and to follow their submission guidelines.

We see examples of interactions that attempt to arouse in the other person an eager want every day. You might think, given that we live in a constant stream of advertisements collectively promising to solve all our problems, that this approach to relationships would be second nature. But it isn't, especially when it comes to promoting our writing. Nothing marks you as an amateur more quickly than a query that focuses on your writing dreams (i.e., your wants) and how the recipient can help you realize them.

The ways in which we can fall into the trap of focusing on our wants in a professional relationship are many, varied, and sometimes subtle. We are, of course, responsible for our own careers. But sometimes we allow that responsibility to become so consuming we project it onto others: our ambition eclipses the other person's wants.

OUR DREAMS AND OTHER PEOPLE'S VALUE

Would-be authors talk about writing the, "break-out," novel—the book that bursts on the national scene to universal acclaim, establishing the author as a major literary figure. There's only one problem with this dream where professional relationships are concerned: it's all about how success would satisfy your wants.

Before you can break out, you've got to write the, "break-in," novel. You've got to show you can deliver a work that other people, who neither know nor care about your ambitions, will find valuable.

There are many areas of endeavor where you've got

to prove your ability before you're given free reign. Why should writing for publication be an exception?

What does it mean to Break In?

When authors tell the story of how they got their books in the bookstores, they often talk in terms of, "breaking into," publishing. (Perhaps that's why we don't laugh when people say that publishing is like a high-security facility.) And because of the way we tell stories (i.e., we skip the boring bits), it's easy to hear breaking-in as synonymous with having arrived.

What does it really mean to break in?

It doesn't mean you've made it.

In the market we call publishing, breaking in means you're now a player because someone is willing to make a non-trivial investment in your work.

- Getting an agent means that he or she is investing their time and energy because they believe they can land a contract for your book and get paid.

- Getting a contract means the publisher is investing real money, both by financing your advance and through the cost they will bear, in your book.

- Getting readers who will buy your book means they are investing some money and, more importantly, time in your story.

In other words, breaking in only means that you're invest-able.

But there are no guarantees—for any of the parties involved—that the investment will pay off.

SHORT-TERM AND LONG-TERM WANTS

We often encourage writers to follow their dreams, reach for the stars, and go for the gusto. Authors, however, who have attained a measure of success, understand passion must be tempered with discipline. Without the care that comes from perspective, we run a real risk of letting our short-term wants undermine our long-range objectives.

Aprilynne Pike recounted her own experience with the temptations that arise when passion shades into desperation:

> "By the time I got an agent, I was basically desperate enough that I probably would have taken any legit agent I could get. By the time I got published, I would have taken just about any legit publisher I could get.

As Pike held out she watched other writers take the first agent or deal they got only to find themselves in places other than where they wanted to be (e.g., a small press, or a genre that wasn't their first love).

> "All of my firsts, set me on the path I want to be in. On the path that fit my goals. But, what was not luck, is that when it became obvious that my book was not going to sell, I looked for another way to meet my goals. I wrote another book. It eventually led me to the career I have now." [5]

Pike didn't let her short-term desire to publish her current book side-track her efforts to find the right agent and publisher to be her partners. More importantly, she didn't let her passion for her current project stop her from setting it aside and moving on to another one that did a better job of arousing an eager want in her readers.

KNOW WHEN TO HOLD 'EM, KNOW WHEN TO FOLD 'EM

How long should you keep pursuing a project?

When does tenacity cease to be a virtue?

How do you know when to set one project aside and invest your energy in something fresh?

At a convention, I was surprised to hear agents on a panel mention projects they'd shopped for years (as in four or five) before finally making a sale. I was under the impression agents generally shop a project for a year or so and then, in the interest of maximizing return on effort (or because they've exhausted their list of potential editors), move on to something else.

On the other hand, publishing is often characterized as essentially a game of persistence: if you keep showing up, you'll eventually get a turn. But no one ever specifies the kind of persistence that pays off. Do you refine and polish your master work—there are a fair number of classics that were decades in the making—or do you persist in producing new projects until you find that one that resonates?

The common answer is that it depends on you and your situation.

That's neither comforting nor helpful.

If you were a rational economic actor, you would watch for the point at which the opportunity costs of not doing something else approach the sunk costs already invested in the project. Or, in colloquial terms, you'd stop when you realize you're throwing good money (or effort) after bad.

I once read about a couple who adopted a rule of three for major expenditures. If one or both of them thought they should buy something they'd postpone the decision to see if they still thought it was a good idea later. They would do this at least twice, on the theory that if the idea came up three times it was probably something they needed and should buy.

My advice, if you're wondering whether to hold or fold a project, is similar (and not unlike the advice to let a draft cool before undertaking revisions): set the project aside for a season. If it's easy to forget, then it's time to be done. If it won't let you go—if it continues to arouse an eager want for you—then you shouldn't let it go either.

* * *

There's a fine line between believing you have something to contribute to the conversation that other people will value and believing you're so good everyone should pay attention to you. We've focused on arousing in the other person an eager want not because the customer is always right but because in a relationship the other person values you to a large degree based on the needs you satisfy.

CHAPTER 15.

AGENTS

"A leprechaun is a type of fairy in Irish folklore, usually taking the form of an old man, clad in a red or green coat, who enjoys partaking in mischief. ... If ever captured by a human, the Leprechaun has the magical power to grant three wishes in exchange for their release." (Wikipedia) [6]

The way many would-be writers talk about their quest to secure an agent implies a fantasy that, once captured, the agent will grant three publishing wishes.

I have some sobering news: agents are not mythical creatures but are, in fact, people too.

What does this mean?

First, agents do not possess publishing magic. Having one does not guarantee publication, though it may help. Getting an agent is generally the precursor to a great deal more work on your part.

Second, as people (not Leprechauns), agents have their own personalities, backgrounds, and biases. You will like some and dislike others. By the same token, some will like you and your work while others won't care for one or both.

A corollary is that there is no universal and objective standard of book goodness to which all agents subscribe; there is no college of agents and publishing professionals who bless or condemn manuscripts; and no matter how great your manuscript may be, some, perhaps most, agents will not offer to represent it.

Third, and most important—as fun and interesting as agents may be as people—at the end of the day the relationship between author and agent is that of a business partnership. Proper partners have something to contribute to each other's business. Between them they can create a whole that feels magical because it is greater than the sum of its parts. The magic, of course, is the product of synergy and a lot of hard work by both parties.

EMPATHY FOR AGENTS

I'm not an agent, and the only kind I play on TV is secret (wait, I've said too much), but I've done enough hiring to empathize with literary agents.

Every time we advertise a job we list a handful of requirements for the position and for the process (e.g., send us a resume). No matter how we phrase the requirements, we inevitably get responses from all over the map:

- Some have nothing to do with the job.
- Some come from people with wildly inappropriate experience (e.g., I've operated a cash register so I can build enterprise software).

- Many come from people who don't follow the simple instructions to include a resume.

- We sometimes receive pitches from applicant's agents, who are also too important to follow our instructions.

There were even people who felt they had to berate us and our flawed decision making process for not recognizing their inherent talent (e.g., "if you had been more diligent, you would have reached a different conclusion,") when we decided they wouldn't be a good fit.

If you replace job application with query does this sound familiar?

Another point that will sound familiar is that I was easily able to dismiss 90% of the responses because it was obvious they hadn't paid attention to either our requirements for the job or the application process. By the same token, it was easy to see who among the respondents had made a good-faith effort and we didn't hold unimportant details like resume format against them.

What does this mean when you're ready to query agents?

First, do yourself and the agents you wish to query a favor and try to follow their submission instructions. Just that much care and attention on your part will put you ahead of 90% of the other people sending queries.

Second, a good faith effort, which includes doing enough research to be confident that the agent actually represents projects like yours, is more important than agonizing over every tiny detail. This is not to say you'll get a pass on grammar and spelling errors. But no agent is going to care whether you indent the first line of each paragraph (which you shouldn't in a standard business letter) if the words in those paragraphs describe a project that fits what they're looking for.

Put another way, what we wanted in response to our job posting wasn't that hard, yet I was amazed at all the ways people found to make it harder. That's why it was refreshing to open a response and see that they'd actually paid attention to our requirements.

Of course, we didn't hire everybody who sent us a good resume. Similarly, no agent is going to respond favorably to every well-crafted, carefully-targeted query.

That said, don't make querying any harder than it needs to be: relax, take a breath, read the instructions twice, and then give it your best shot.

QUERIES ODDS

As a rule of thumb, an agent will find one client out of every four or five thousand queries. [7]

I'll let you take a moment to get over the shock of the apparent odds of 1 in 4000.

Now let me try to help you restore some equanimity.

Many agents say at least 90% of the queries they receive are non-starters: the query is addressed to, "Dear Agent," or to the agent and hundreds of other agents; it's a genre the agent doesn't represent; the word count is outside industry norms; the author sounds desperate, crazy, or both; and so on. If 90% of the queries are non-starters, then the odds for your well-crafted query sent to well-researched agents are more in the neighborhood of 400 to 1.

400 to 1 isn't great, but it also isn't terrible. If you

look at it as purely a numbers game, it simply means that you've got to send about 400 queries.

But before you fire up your trusty spam generator, consider that there are probably only about a hundred agents who might be interested in a given project. You can't query those hundred agents four times unless you have four different projects. The good news is that four seems to be the average number of novels people write before they get published.

I wouldn't blame you if, at this point, you're still a bit discouraged: the numbers seem stacked against you unless you're willing to put in a great deal of effort over the long term. That, however, is exactly what is required if you want to write for a broad audience.

ON THE SPREAD OF THE, "NO RESPONSE MEANS NO," POLICY

"Don't call us, we'll call you."

It's the classic Hollywood line—the epitome of Tinsel Town, that city of dreams built atop a mountain of broken ones. While we might be tempted to look down on callous film people, they're simply responding as rational economic actors in the presence of a dramatic oversupply of dramatic talent.

And now, more and more agents are going Hollywood: not that they're turning to film but that they're adopting an analogous query policy where no response means no. The more thoughtful agents have set up email auto-responders so that writers can know their query didn't get lost in a spam filter and have a publicly stated response time frame after which authors can assume the response is, "no thanks."

The **Society of Children's Book Writers and**

Illustrators (SCBWI) weighed in with an open letter asking agents to reconsider their policy. Among other things, the SCBWI worried that the policy would not help agents reduce their query load because the absence of feedback encourages writers to treat querying as a numbers game instead of targeting submissions after careful research.

Much of the ensuing discussion revolved around the question of what was right: if writers put lots of time into their query, weren't they owed the courtesy of a response?

While I would like to think that the industry still has the civility to cloak self-interest behind the decency of encouraging professional development, at a purely economic level the, "no response means no," policy simply means that agents now have an oversupply of queries.

What caused the oversupply?

Perhaps the number of writers querying publishable manuscripts has grown dramatically in the last few years.

Perhaps the commercial market for debut authors has contracted.

So what should you do?

It's hard to resist the temptation to treat querying as a numbers game where you fire-and-forget at all the agents who seem to be in the ball park. But without feedback, you won't be able to refine your query after each small batch.

There is, however, a deeper question: can you stand out in an oversupplied market? Or should you, perhaps, look elsewhere, either to other agents who haven't instituted the policy or to other publishing avenues?

CARE AND FEEDING

And what if you do land an agent?

All living things, of which a professional relationship is one, require care and feeding. Lest that makes agents sound too much like house plants, let me hasten to add that the care in this case is managing expectations and feeding is communication.

One of the very first things to work out with an agent, even before you accept an offer of representation, is how you will communicate. Everyone has a different style—some people want to know every detail, some only want to hear about important matters. Regardless of your preferences, a clear understanding from the very beginning of how and when you will communicate is the foundation for a successful and mutually satisfying relationship.

As much as the process of finding an agent feels like auditioning with your fingers crossed, hoping they'll take you on, the fact of the matter is that once you agree to let an agent represent your work, they're working for you—not for you exclusively but they are working for you. It's more than a partnership because an agent represents your interests and has a fiduciary duty to you. Insofar as your relationship is concerned, it is your responsibility to let your agent know if you are unhappy about anything in as timely and clear a fashion as possible.

There's an old story about a fellow who gets a flat tire while driving in the country. It's dusk and he has no jack. He sets off, cursing his bad luck, to march up the road to the last farm house he passed a mile to two back. Like the evening, his mood grows darker as he worries about how late it is, how late he is, how upset the farmer will be when he wakes them up, how much trouble it will be to change the tire in the dark, and so on. By the time he gets to the now dark farm house, he's in such a state that he bounds onto the porch, hammers on the door, and shouts, "I don't want your damn jack!"

You might laugh, or at least smile, at the motorist, but I suspect most of us have done the same at one time or another. The mistake here is to let your unilateral expectations get out of hand. The farmer may have been perfectly willing to help once the motorist had explained his plight. Instead, by assuming the farmer would act a certain way, the motorist acted to turn his fears into a self-fulfilling prophesy.

Many writers undermine their professional relationships because they let their fears manage their expectations. They're in good company with any number of other people—which is all the more tragic because by virtue of their art they possess a tool that could help them avoid this pitfall: empathy. In the same way that your empathy enables you to get into the head of even the most odious character and understand them well enough to give them a vivid rendering on the page, you should be able to put yourself in the place of the other parties in your professional relationships and see how their behavior toward you is almost certainly not malicious. (Indeed, the most likely explanation for most of the unpleasant things that might come up in a relationship is that the other party was simply oblivious of you, your needs, or how their actions might affect you.)

The single most important technique for managing expectations, both your own and those of the other party, is to assume nothing. Always check and double-check your understanding with your partner. And when you do so, never assume anything other than a neutral tone. Ask any questions clearly and without prejudice.

Remember, the hallmark of a professional is that you don't create problems but instead employ all your capacities to solve them. If you build an even-keeled approach atop the foundation of communication you took care to establish at the beginning of the relationship, you'll go far because people will enjoy working with you.

CHAPTER 16.

CARNEGIE'S SIX WAYS TO MAKE PEOPLE LIKE YOU

You can't, in fact, make people like you. What you can do, however, is make yourself more likable. Carnegie offers six techniques through which you can improve your likability.

ONE: BECOME GENUINELY INTERESTED IN OTHER PEOPLE

One of the aphorisms my mother often shared with me was, "People don't care how much you know until they know how much you care."

Even though writing is mostly a solitary pursuit there are thousands of ways to become genuinely interested in other people.

Here are a few examples to get you started.

- **Fellow writers** – get involved in local writing groups; listen to what other writers have to say; offer to read and comment on their manuscripts.

- **Authors** – get to know the authors in your area and your genre; read their books; go to conferences and signings and meet them.

- **Professionals** – get to know some publishing professionals. Blogs by agents, editors, and publishers are a great way to get at least some sense of who these people are, what they're interested in, and what concerns they have.

- **Like-minded People** – blogging is not about self-promotion. Find like-minded people on the Internet and listen to what they have to say; make helpful, constructive comments on their blogs; and invite people to participate in the blogs and forums you host.

- **Readers** – if you hope to get paid for your work you should be genuinely interested in your readers and spend a major portion of your outreach efforts trying to find out who they are and what they like.

And if you're still not convinced you should be genuinely interested in other people, consider this: all human groups have signs they use to distinguish members from non-members. While the specifics differ from group to group, knowing the names of key members is a nearly universal way to show that you're part of the group.

TWO: SMILE

I scoffed the first time I heard that the phone company (yes, back when there was only one) trained its operators to smile when they spoke with customers. It seemed pointless if no one could see them. But because smiling changes the shape of the face and the vocal tract, you really can hear the difference.

Smiles are inherently disarming. Anthropologists speculate that hominids showed their teeth without exposing their canines to signal non-aggressive interaction. As simple as it is, meeting someone with a smile immediately changes the tenor of the interaction.

"Okay," you say, "as an author, I can manage a smile when I'm in public."

That's a good start. Smile at everyone who comes to a signing, reading, or presentation. It's a small way to give honest, sincere appreciation to the people who have been generous enough to come and spend some time with you.

But much of your time as an author will be solitary. Does the advice still apply?

First, and foremost, smiling even when there's no one else to see is good for your mental and physical well-being. This may sound strange, but not only do I feel better when I smile, it feels like the words come a bit easier. Clearly a smile by itself won't cure an illness, nor will it cause you to pour out a flawless novel, but it will make it better.

Second, readers can hear the smile (or its absence) in your writing. I'm not talking about overtly sunny writing: smiling doesn't mean you're limited to rainbows and ponies. We talk—often obsess—about an author's voice. Just like a spoken voice, a smile comes through as part of your written voice, particularly in terms of the enthusiasm with which you tell the story.

And if none of that moves you, you should, at the very least, practice smiling during the lonely hours so that when you must be seen in public your facial muscles will be able to manage more than a grotesque grimace that frightens children and small animals.

THREE: REMEMBER A PERSON'S NAME

People are fundamentally self-centered. Noble aspirations and modern astronomy notwithstanding, we are each walking Ptolemaic systems: we are the centers of our universes.

Using a person's name gives you a direct channel into the heart of their universe.

So what practical benefit does this principle have for writers?

First, learning and using the names of the people (like agents and editors) with whom you want to do business is more than professional courtesy: it signals that you're likely to take at least some of their interests into account. This is why botching a name or using a generic salutation like, "Dear Agent," in a query is generally a major strike against you.

Second, even in public situations like signings, where most of us have no hope of remembering the names of all the people we meet, using the name of the person with whom you're speaking after you learn it is the conversational equivalent of a smile: it's a verbal token that says, "I recognize you."

FOUR: BE A GOOD LISTENER

Unless you've been living under a social media rock, you know that relentless self promotion is the surest way to alienate people. Instead, we're encouraged to get out and interact, leaving, for example, thoughtful, relevant comments on blogs. Of course, you need to listen to the conversation for a while to determine which of the things you want to say might be relevant.

I've heard several people suggest the ratio of your ears to your mouth is a good guideline for the proportion of listening to talking.

Listening and encouraging others to talk about themselves is even more important at conferences and events with publishing professionals. While you should have something to say for yourself—an introduction and a brief answer/pitch for the inevitable, "Oh, and what do you write?" question—you'll get much more out of encouraging others to talk about themselves.

Unconvinced?

Dale Carnegie tells a story of a salesman who asked a few questions and then spent most of his appointment listening. A few days later, the prospect placed a large order because the salesman was, "such a nice young man."

Put in more concrete terms, no agent or editor is going to fall in love with your manuscript based on your interactions at a conference, but they will be more interested in your project if you showed your interest in them by being a good listener.

Finally, at the broadest level, you need to listen to the market—not to chase trends, but to meet the market half way. There are any number of ways to listen to the market—blogs, reviews, studying bookstores—but the single most valuable way you can listen to the market and encourage books to talk about themselves is to read them.

FIVE: TALK IN THE TERMS OF THE OTHER PERSON'S INTEREST

This may seem a bit redundant in light of what we've

discussed so far, but it goes to the heart of what it means to be a writer.

AGENTS

Telling an agent how they can help you fulfill your dreams of publication is an excellent example of how not to talk in terms of the other person's interest.

What is in an agent's interest?

An agent wants to find books that will sell and earn him or her a nice commission.

Your interests, aside from producing a book that will sell, are largely irrelevant to them. Indeed, in the early stages, all an agent really wants to know about you is that you're not crazy and won't be too painful to work with.

EDITORS AND OTHER INDUSTRY PROFESSIONALS

Your interests and those of editors and other industry professionals have an even smaller overlap than the interests of you and your agent. Editors are interested in the particular project they've bought and care about your interests only to the degree that they help move the project through publication and out into the market.

Communicating in a professional, business-like manner is the best way to talk primarily in terms of the other person's interest.

READERS

To this point, the suggestions have been fairly straightforward—perhaps even standard practice for good interpersonal skills. But when we turn our attention to readers, we find something wonderful.

The main thing that distinguishes writers from other

people who put words on the page is that writers talk in the terms of readers' interests.

Think about it.

The only reason anyone parts with his or her hard-earned cash and devotes hours to your book is because they believe it addresses their interests. From entertainment to information, readers only care about what's in it for them.

SIX: MAKE THE OTHER PERSON FEEL IMPORTANT AND DO IT SINCERELY

This one is a challenge, and no mistake, because it doesn't work without sincerity. Carnegie tells of a party where he was cornered by a bore. He had to look long and hard to find something he could say with sincerity, but at length he said, "You're clearly someone who is passionate about this subject, and that's something I admire."

One of the simplest ways to make someone feel important is to give honest and sincere appreciation. An expression of appreciation acknowledges that the other person exists and is valued—the cornerstone of feeling important.

Another general approach, as illustrated by Carnegie's example, is to find something you sincerely admire about the other person and share your opinion with them.

A thoughtful note or gesture, particularly in professional relationships where such things are not expected, goes a long way to helping a person with whom you deal (like your agent, editor, or publicist) feel important in a good way. Of course, it must be sincere, which generally means it must be personal.

So as a writer, what can you do to make people feel important?

Some writers have a knack for making each and every person in line at a signing feel important. One, for example, thanked each person and asked if he could take their picture holding the book. It takes stamina to greet the 237th person as warmly as the first, but it's worth it.

And in terms of what you actually write, the best stories are told with a voice that whispers, "You, dear reader, are so important I wrote this for you."

An interesting side effect with this technique is that the more you sincerely make the other person feel important, the more important you become to them.

CHAPTER 17.

AUDIENCE

As a writer, there are many people on whom you should use Carnegie's techniques, but one group is far and away more important than all others: your audience.

Does that mean dropping whatever you thought you might do and going for what seems popular? That strategy seems like it might be in line with the advice to become genuinely interested in other people, talk in terms of their interest, and make them feel important. In other words, is the customer always right?

Your job as a writer is to bring something new to the conversation. And do it in a way that addresses the needs of your readers. Now that you understand Carnegie's six techniques you can apply them to the problem of finding your audience.

WHERE TO START?

The genre into which your book falls is one of the basic pieces of information you're supposed to include in your query.

For a long time I thought about genre in library

terms—that is, as a way of organizing a collection of materials. When I visit the library, liking a book is a secondary (or tertiary) concern, well behind basic questions like, "Does it provide the information I need?" Even with fiction, I survey the shelves and then scan the books, looking at more than the first page, to determine my interest.

In a book store, however, the fiction buyer is generally there to find something they like, not to survey the offerings. With the exception of mega-best-sellers that become independent cultural forces, not everyone will like your work.

In fact, most people won't.

Thanks to the practical matter of only having twenty four hours in a day, I don't *like* about 95% of what's in the book store—it's not a matter of whether it's good or bad, it's simply that I don't have time to pay attention to all that material. By the same logic, 95% of the people won't *like* your work.

That realization lead to an epiphany: getting published is really about finding an audience.

Notions like genre are at best an approximation of an audience. So are all the rules and expectations of genres and commercial publishing. The zeal with which the gatekeepers sometimes seem to uphold these rules only shows their best guesses as to what a given audience wants.

So what does all this mean?

You will be on a much more positive footing with both gatekeepers and the buying public if you don't try to please everybody but look instead for the people with whom your work resonates.

DEMYSTIFYING GENRE

Marion Jensen said, "When you pick a genre, you've got to pick something that you like. It's kind of like picking a career."

Just like the end of high school, when well-meaning parents and counselors say, in effect, "Now that you've spent your life listening to us tell you what to do, it's time for you to decide what you want to do—oh and by the way, this decision will have life-long consequences," you've got to decide something you can't truly understand until you've lived with your decision.

The good news is that choosing the genre in which you'll write is a critical decision only if you succeed.

Why?

Because with each book you publish you create precedents and build expectations among your growing circle of readers. It's not that you can never try anything different, but imagine the hue and cry if J. K. Rowling decided she wanted to write erotica.

The advice about picking a genre is better understood in terms of setting up shop someplace where you're comfortable because you could be spending a lot of time there.

One of the reasons this seems like a big deal is because *genre* is to *kind* as *veal* is to *beef*. This is another in a long series of cases where we have two words in English with the same meaning, but the Latinate, or more specifically French, version sounds more sophisticated.

Repeat after me, "Genre means kind." It's no more or less complicated than deciding the kind of books with which your book ought to be grouped.

And why does that matter?

Because you're hoping to take advantage of recommendation engines, whether human or automatic, that will suggest someone might like your book if they liked something similar.

Put another way, in terms of publishing being a market, genre is shorthand for your audience.

That's the real reason why you must decide on your genre: you must know your audience and their expectations.

HOW TO FOLLOW TRENDS

It takes about two years to go from manuscript to publication. What's hot now is practically guaranteed to be dull by then—which is why you'll always be late to the table if you write to trends.

The best, and most consistent, advice is to write a story you love instead of chasing the market. There will always be a market for a good story.

So as we write, driven only by the pure flame of inspiration, can we safely ignore trends?

For the most part.

Your job is to meet the market half-way. In order to do that, you must have some sense as to where the market is and where it seems to be going. For example, if you were an auto maker, would now, with the price of gas rising, growing concerns about our dependence on foreign oil, and a strong green movement, be a good time to introduce a monster truck whose fuel economy is measured in gallons per mile? By the same token, in a market glutted with vampire stories, should you really try to do one more? Or is there, perhaps some other under-appreciated paranormal type that sucks away your life (like lawyers) with which you could do something fresh?

In terms of market awareness, there's some value in being aware of trends. But there's a big difference between being aware and following.

So is there any time you should actually follow a trend?

Yes, but only when you're currently shopping a manuscript and can use the trend to help position your piece. If, say, you've written about sparkly, salmon merfolk and their eternal battle with the were-bears, and if you learn that an editor wants a paranormal fish story, you should waste no time crafting a query that says, "I've got just what you're looking for!"

CATERING TO VERSUS CREATING AN AUDIENCE

Writing in *Electronic Musician*, Steven Wilson said, "This, for me, is the distinction between an entertainer (cater to an audience) and an artist (create your own audience)."

Wilson's distinction is enlightening, not because the artist is more noble than the entertainer but because of the way in which it clarifies the nature of the audiences.

This is not about selling out or maintaining artistic integrity. You must meet the market half-way whether you're catering to an audience or creating one:

- In the catering case, you've got to bring something new to the existing audience: without some variations on the theme, they'll get bored and go elsewhere. You need something that will compel them to pay attention to your project.

- In the creating case, you've got to frame your novelties in familiar terms so that the audience you attract can get their bearings. You need to entice them to explore something new.

How do you know what kind of audience you should address?

If you're writing something that fits comfortably in one genre, like epic fantasy, where readers' expectations are fairly clear, the audience expects you to cater to them. If you're writing something that mixes genres, you'll likely have to create an audience.

Think about what you're trying to do. Now think about how your audience will find you. The distinction between the entertainer and the artist will help clarify the issues.

FIRST IMPRESSIONS

I once participated in a first page critique session with an agent at a writing conference. I came away convinced that it was an exercise of limited utility: if you're looking for problems, you can likely find something in just about anyone's 250-word sample, particularly if you read it without any other context.

Clearly, first impressions matter. Readers won't keep reading if the story doesn't start in an interesting place. Indeed, readers won't even pick up the book if nothing about it piques their curiosity or stirs their interest. But first impressions only matter to a point.

Malcolm Gladwell argues for first impressions in his book *Blink*. He calls it, "rapid cognition," (which sounds better than, "go with your gut,") and claims our first reaction is often the right one. This is generally the case for agents and editors when looking at bad writing. But it's not true for good writing: you can't tell whether the entire book will be good from a one-page sample.

What if you want to do something that plays off of first impressions? When the pilot for *Babylon 5* aired, a critic called it a ho-hum, me-too space opera with over-the-top characterization: the villain and the comic relief character were obvious. But over the course of the series, those two characters (and all the others) developed in ways perfectly consistent with their behavior in the pilot that completely contradicted the critic's first impressions. The payoff came only for those willing to get past their first impressions.

So what does this mean?

As a reader, you must resist the temptation to assume you know what the book is about after you read the first page or the first chapter.

And as a writer, you've got to make things compelling enough to carry people past their first impressions.

HOW DO YOU ENCOURAGE READER INTEREST?

We all have books we like only because we forced ourselves to keep reading. Similarly, we all have books we don't like because we forced ourselves to keep reading. In both cases, our feelings are stronger because of the effort we put into reading the book.

Clearly, you'll never sell anything that is impenetrable (unless you're named James Joyce) and we all want a story that pulls the reader effortlessly along, but it's easy to go too far making the story easy on the reader when we ought to focus on making it compelling.

Readers will persist if they have some interest. I've read books whose hook, blurb, or artwork fired my imagination. I've read books whose story pulled me in at some point. And I've read books for market research that I would have abandoned if I had been reading for pleasure. In all these cases, I read the entire book because I had a compelling interest.

What's tricky about reader interest is that there's only so much a writer can do. Reader interest can be enhanced or suppressed by external factors. How many times have you read something, not because of something about the book itself but because everyone is talking about it and you have to know too?

So what can you do?

There are no silver bullets or special trick. Carnegie's six techniques—become genuinely interested in other people, smile, remember a person's name, be a good listener, talk in terms of the other person's interest, and make the other person feel important—give you a framework for encouraging reader interest. All the tools of your craft, all the rules of writing, and all red marks from the editor help to avoid discouraging reader interest, but in order to encourage them to read you must do the hard work of getting past yourself as the author and become genuinely interested in your readers and what interests them.

SELF-CONSCIOUS OF YOUR AUDIENCE

Martin Amis said:

> "People ask me if I ever thought of writing a children's book ... I say, 'If I had a serious brain injury I might well write a children's book', but otherwise the idea of being conscious of who you're directing the story to is anathema to me, because, in my view, fiction is freedom and any restraints on that are intolerable. ... I would never write about someone that forced me to write at a lower register than what I can write." [8]

Madeleine L'Engle said:

"You have to write the book that wants to be written. And if the book will be too difficult for grown-ups, then you write it for children."

But there's something deeper than calling out someone for literary arrogance at work here. Amis said, "... the idea of being conscious of who you're directing the story to is anathema to me." In children's literature, the worst examples of talking down to children come from authors who are conscious—or, more to the point, self-conscious—of their audience.

So does that mean Amis is right? That you should be unconscious of your audience?

No, quite the opposite.

You need to know your audience so well that addressing them in appropriate and evocative ways is simply second nature. One of the hallmarks of a master is how they make what they do look easy—as if they didn't give it a second thought.

Amis can say, "fiction is freedom and any restraints on that are intolerable," because he knows his current audience so well that he is effectively unconscious of them, and he can say he would, "never write about someone that forced me to write at a lower register than what I can write," because coming to know another, younger audience would, for him, be a process full of self-conscious restraints.

Children's authors feel none of the restraints that worry Amis because they don't talk to their audience, they talk with them. And the very best are, themselves, still very much a part of their audience.

CHAPTER 18.

CARNEGIE'S TWELVE WAYS TO WIN PEOPLE TO YOUR WAY OF THINKING

Convincing someone to invest ten hours in reading your words is fundamentally about wining people to your way of thinking. The people who become your readers do so because they want to hear your story in your voice, all of which is a product of your way of thinking.

ONE: AVOID ARGUMENTS

How often have you felt compelled to read a book—perhaps because everyone else is talking about it and you don't want to be left out?

I often don't enjoy the thing that is popular because very few works can meet the expectations created by that much hype. Or, in Carnegie's terms, I've not been won to the author's way of thinking; rather I've lost an, "argument," with popular opinion.

Arguments are about compulsion, which will never truly win anyone to your way of thinking. This is particularly true for writers who receive criticism or rejections from writing groups, agents, editors, or reviewers. Arguing that the person making the criticism doesn't, "get it," isn't going to help them, "get it." They'll simply dig in and redouble their opposition.

The best policy is to listen and learn. You may need clarification, but take care that your request for clarification doesn't put the other party on the defensive.

TWO: SHOW RESPECT FOR THE OTHER PERSON'S OPINIONS. NEVER TELL SOMEONE THEY ARE WRONG

This principle flows naturally from the first. Telling someone they are wrong is the first salvo in an argument.

Notice, by the way, that the key word here is *opinions*. If it truly is a matter of fact (and very few thing are), and the error could cause harm, that's another case. But publishing is a deeply subjective business—which is a diplomatic way to say that nobody really knows what works in an objective or, more importantly, predictive sense.

This principle is particularly important to remember when dealing with rejection. First, once someone has decided they can't sell your project, that opinion becomes their truth and you won't get their best efforts if you force the issue. Second, with the knowledge that it is the other person's opinion, you can move on confident that the rejection is not an objective condemnation but simply means it wasn't the right project for them.

THREE: IF YOU'RE WRONG, ADMIT IT QUICKLY AND EMPHATICALLY

Admitting your mistakes quickly and emphatically is a good idea for many reasons, the most important of which is that it's a powerful way to defuse a potentially confrontational situation.

As a writer, admitting your errors demonstrates a fundamental willingness to learn and improve. That willingness should apply to both your craft and the conduct of your public relationships.

In terms of what we do as writers, consider this: the most interesting protagonists are not perfect. As the protagonist of your own story, you don't have to be perfect either. Indeed, our culture generally views someone who is candid about their shortcomings far more charitably than someone who denies they have short comings.

FOUR: BEGIN IN A FRIENDLY WAY

This principle is best illustrated in terms of queries. Among sure-fire query turn-offs, a diatribe about how everything published prior to your book is rubbish, how the industry is broken because they haven't recognized your genius, or a promise that this is the agent's lucky day because your project is destined for such mind-boggling success that it won't be long before people say, "J.K. Rowling? Who's that?" are all near the top of the list.

Beginning in a friendly way, whether in person or on paper with a query, is simply saying, in effect, "I recognize you're a decent person. I hope you can see that I'm a decent person too."

Put another way, a friend is someone who is aware of some of your needs and interests, and who, by implied social covenant, will not take advantage of that knowledge. That's a powerful foundation upon which to establish a relationship.

FIVE: START WITH QUESTIONS THE OTHER PERSON WILL ANSWER YES TO

Using a rhetorical question in a query, particularly one that the agent might answer with a, "no," is a bad idea. If you begin a query with, "Have you ever wondered what would happen if a hippopotamus appeared in your bathroom?" and the agent answers, "no," you're pretty much dead in the water.

The more often we say, "Yes," to someone, the more likely we are to agree with them. The converse is equally true. You've likely experienced a crude form of this with hard-selling telemarketers when they say something like, "Do you want to save money?" (How often have you had the strength of will to say, "No, not if it means working with you.")

While a conversation might afford you an opportunity to get an agent or editor to say, "Yes," doing so in a written form is more subtle because you don't have the advantage of interaction (e.g., the opportunity to ask a question again). Still there are implicit questions you can help your reader answer with a yes:

- Does this writer have a command of the English language?
- Have they taken care to correct typos and errors?
- Have they told me the name of their project and given me some basic information like genre, audience, and word count?
- Can they convey what their book is about in a few paragraphs?

- Do they understand that a query is a business letter and not a confessional?

The same care and attention in all your writing will help readers say yes to your books.

SIX: LET THE OTHER PERSON DO THE TALKING

People care first and foremost about their own needs. Listening, of course, is a good way to learn about those needs, but this principle goes beyond listening. A person who sells themselves on something is much more committed to the product or idea than someone who gets talked into it.

In writing, this means that the reader's experience with the project itself is the most powerful way to win them over. Hence the oft repeated advice to write the very best books you can and make other considerations, like promotion, a lower priority.

In more concrete terms, this is why you generally want to show, not tell. By showing, you help the reader tell themselves the story.

SEVEN: LET THE OTHER PERSON FEEL THE IDEA IS HIS OR HERS

At one level, this principle comes down to proper deportment in our society. Whether in person or online, blatant self-promotion comes across as unseemly. Assuring an agent in your query that you are the next undiscovered writing superstar will put you on the fast track to rejection.

Proper deportment, by the way, is another reason you may want an agent. They can say they think your book will be big when they pitch to an editor because in the social equation they are a, "disinterested," third party.

But there's something deeper at work here: people are always much more passionate about their own ideas than those they adopt from other people.

EIGHT: TRY HONESTLY TO SEE THINGS FROM THE OTHER PERSON'S POINT OF VIEW

The applications of this principle in personal relations should be fairly obvious. But it's easy to loose sight of it when you run into opposition.

When you receive a rejection, put on your agent hat and consider why you might reject your own query.

When your editor asks for a change you're reluctant to make, try to imagine why you might ask for the same change if you were in his or her shoes.

But the most important application of this principle as a writer is to try to see your writing from the point of view of your reader. If you didn't know the cool stuff that comes later, would this scene still feel like it's advancing the story? Does the reader really need to know the history of your world when they're still trying to figure out who the main characters are?

NINE: SYMPATHIZE WITH THE OTHER PERSON

A sympathetic approach to a point of contention can go a long way toward smoothing over the situation. Even though it may be difficult to believe the publisher who just proposed a truly atrocious cover is on your side, the fact is that you both want the book to do well. Approaching the editor with an expression that shows you sympathize with the efforts they're making on your behalf given the constraints under which they operate is much more effective than throwing a tantrum about their lack of design sense.

More importantly, writers should sympathize with their readers. Many of the rules of writing can be reduced to asking yourself, "Am I writing this because it will help my reader enjoy the story, or am I writing it to show off?"

TEN: APPEAL TO NOBLE MOTIVES

Carnegie explains that appealing to the person someone imagines themselves to be is an effective way to motivate people. He uses example phrases like, "Because I know you're an honest person ...," to show how such an appeal is both disarming and enabling.

Of course, starting a query with something like, "Dear Ms. Agent, because I know you to be a person of such impeccable taste that you will instantly see the superior merit of my book ...," is almost certain not to produce the desired effect.

This principle has a more subtle application for writers. Done right, we invite people to become better by reading our books. The potential self-improvement might be more obvious with non-fiction, but fiction offers the improvement that comes through experiencing and understanding the story.

Why do readers spend their time with our fiction? They want to step away from their common concerns and experience something different. Even if your characters and their actions are anything but noble, the catharsis of a well-told tale is still ennobling.

And in terms of craft, the characters that populate our work should have something admirable about them. Even the most black-hearted villain has, at very least, an admirable tenacity.

ELEVEN: DRAMATIZE YOUR IDEAS

In a general sense, this principle echoes the mantra of the writer, "Show, don't tell." Dramatizing, or showing, does two important things:

1. It allows the other person to experience the idea, and
2. It enables the other person to come to their own conclusions about the idea.

Dramatizing your ideas is a powerful way to follow principle seven, "Let the other person feel the idea is his or hers." Enticing someone to adopt your idea creates a far stronger commitment than compelling them to accept the idea.

As a writer, it's a skill you need to master at every level, from your novel to your query. Indeed, you could make a fine case that dramatizing ideas is the heart and soul of what we as writers do.

TWELVE: THROW DOWN A CHALLENGE AND DON'T TALK NEGATIVE WHEN THE PERSON IS ABSENT, TALK ABOUT ONLY POSITIVE

This principle may sound most like a motivational technique: in Carnegie's book he gives an example of a supervisor who set up a contest to see which shift was more productive instead of yelling at the workers to work harder.

What does this have to do with writing?

Consider this: What's the purpose of the hook? Or the title? Or the cover? Or the back cover copy? All of these, at a fundamental level, throw down a challenge to potential readers—something like, "I'll bet you want to find out what this is all about."

A well crafted story delivers challenge after challenge in the form of interesting characters, twisting plots, and rising tension, all of which entice the reader onward.

* * *

Just as you can't make people like you, you can only make yourself more likable, you can't force people to accept your ideas, you can only make your ideas more appealing.

The techniques outlined in this section show how avoiding confrontation, establishing rapport through empathy, and allowing the other person to arrive at the same conclusion all help make your ideas more appealing. For both fiction and non-fiction, it's much easier to win readers to your way of thinking by enticing them to adopt your way of thinking than compelling them to do so.

CHAPTER 19.

MARKETING AND PROMOTION

Why do you choose to read a given book?

All the reasons you might give can be reduced to either you felt compelled or enticed. (Actually, our reasons can be spread along a spectrum from compelled to enticed, but it's easier to talk in terms of dichotomies than the fine shades in a spectrum.)

Books that become a cultural phenomenon (i.e., most people have at least heard of them), do so on the strength of social compulsion. How many times have you picked up a book because everyone else was talking about it and you didn't want to be left out of the conversation?

As writers, there's nothing we can do to cause our books to become a social phenomenon. So the more interesting question is, how, given the means in our power, can we appeal to readers?

We can pitch our books as either compelling or enticing. A compelling pitch usually centers on a situation or issue the reader might confront. There's an immediate identification because it's in the world of our common experience. An enticing pitch plays on mystery, wonder, intrigue, or, as the kids say, something cool. There's a fascination because it's outside the world of our common experience.

Reviewing a list of recommended young adult novels, I noticed a pattern: the realistic stories had compelling pitches and the fantastic stories had enticing pitches. The former suggested, "This could happen to you," while the latter asked, "Wouldn't it be cool if this happened?"

There is, or course, no rule requiring compelling pitches for one genre and enticing pitches for another. In fact, many stories have a mix of compelling and enticing elements. That said, you will find your marketing efforts come more naturally if you understand where your story falls on the spectrum between compelling and enticing.

WHAT'S IT ABOUT?

A writer considering a new project and a reader considering whether to read a new book are both confronted with the same question: "Is it worth my time?"

For the reader, it's only a matter of eight to ten hours. For the writer, the number of hours invested is on the order of hundreds. How can you get some reassurance that your project is worth all that writing time?

If someone recommends a book, your first question as a potential reader is likely, "What's it about?"

While it doesn't guarantee success, if you can answer that question you probably have something worth undertaking.

The holy grail of what's-it-about-ness is a single line that captures the essence and the enticement of the book. You might have heard it called a one-line pitch, a log-line (from film), or a hook. Beware, though, because the kind of hook we're talking about has more than one sharp edge. First, like poetry and other concise art forms, they're hard to do well. Second, if you do come up with a stunning hook it's hard to resist the temptation to think your job is done. (*Snakes on a Plane*, need I say more?) Third, you may come up with a line that's perfect—if you already know the story—but doesn't say a lot to new readers. You could, for example, say Harry Potter is about a lightning-shaped scar: that line packs loads of meaning if you know the series, but isn't very compelling if you know nothing about the story.

You're on firmer ground if you have a synopsis, outline, or even a story bible. But these exercises come with the attendant distraction of all the cool things you're going to include in the book, and you're liable to sound like a four-year-old when you talk about it ("… and it has this, and this, and this, and this …"). Once again, you'll miss the what's-it-about mark, this time with too much information.

Caveats about its reliability aside, my favorite framework is Wikipedia, specifically the notion of writing a Wikipedia entry for your book. Every article on Wikipedia begins with a few paragraphs summarizing the subject. Where the article covers a book, the introductory paragraphs include a few lines describing what the book is about. The articles often also include a synopsis, so it's instructive to find a few entries that do a good job of capturing books with which you are familiar and study both sections.

To be clear, this is a completely private exercise: while you may be able to use some of your material when it comes time to market the book, its primary value is in helping you to develop a clear and compelling mental model of your story.

Your goal is to discover the glowing ember—the combustible combination of concept and passion—of your story that is the essence of what it's about. That essence, even if it changes over time, will guide you as you work through the project and then work to find ways to share it with readers.

MARKETING BEFORE AND AFTER THE FACT

Of all the exotic animals Dr. Doolittle met in his adventures, the pushmi-pullyu (pronounced, 'push-me—pull-you') ranks high on my list of favorites. It was a gazelle-unicorn cross with two heads (and no tail) that often had trouble deciding which way to go.

At first I was going to use the pushmi-pullyu as a mascot for indecisiveness in the publishing industry. But it's a much better analogy for having it both ways—something that's also endemic in publishing, particularly where marketing is concerned.

For a variety of structural reasons (some of which stem from the quarterly pressure to deliver profits to corporate masters and some from the big release model that works best for large chain bookstores), publishing's promotional Holy Grail is *before-the-fact* marketing: a confluence of buzz and publicity that has people lined up to buy the book at midnight when it's released. Similarly, publishers love nothing better than an author who is so well established that the phrase, "The next big-name-author book is out," is enough to make people pull out their credit cards.

Then there are the books that sell year after year with no visible marketing. These books are marketed *after-the-fact* by word of mouth: rather than saying, "The author is good so his or her new book will be good," they can say, "This is a good book—I know: I've read it." The book, by the fact of its existence and availability, can essentially market itself: rather than having to take the opinion of thought leaders on faith, an interested reader can see for themselves.

Once upon a time, publishers made most of their money from their backlist, which provided consistent returns each year without a great deal of marketing effort. Then structural changes shifted the emphasis to first the front list and then the blockbuster. The new model depends upon turning the publication of a book into an event and creating a sense of urgency—which worked when there were fewer channels and distractions.

Now, with a never-ending parade of distractions, the backlist is making a big comeback because the only way to win through the Internoise is with constancy. A publicist recently said, "I'm counseling authors to approach publicity as a long-term, on-going strategy." In other words, successful publicity in the twenty-first century isn't about making a big splash; it's about a constant stream of enticing content.

The challenge for contemporary writers is that the major publishers now want projects that they can sell both *before-the-fact* with a blockbuster push and *after-the-fact* by keeping electronic rights in perpetuity. That's why the industry feels increasingly like a pushmi-pullyu. And that's why it's increasingly the author's responsibility to understand the business implications of *before-the-fact* and *after-the-fact* marketing so that they can make the best deals in light of the short and long term trade-offs.

PROMOTION IS AN EXPRESSION OF GRATITUDE

Authors often wince when they come to understand just

how much they need to promote their work. I confess to being in that camp, particularly when it sounds like we're expected to go out and convince people to read our books.

Kevin Smokler, co-founder and CEO of **BookTour.com**, sees promotion as an expression of gratitude. "Promotion," he says, is primarily "an opportunity to meet people who are interested in your book and thank them for their interest." [9]

Successful promotion comes down to three things:

- A clear message of what it's about
- A way to entice or compel potential readers to pay attention
- Honest and sincere expressions of appreciation for readers' time and attention

There are, of course, entire volumes dedicated to the who, what, and how of promotional campaigns. With all the advice and techniques, it's easy to lose sight of the fundamental fact that promotion is essentially a courtesy for potential readers. If you place the needs of potential readers above your own needs, instead of the slimy taint of salesmanship your promotional efforts will be acts of graciousness.

CHAPTER 20.

AUTHOR PLATFORMS IN THE AGE OF ABUNDANCE

In the there's-no-pleasing-some-advice-givers department, first we were told that prospective authors needed a web presence and now we're supposed to have an *authentic* web presence.

What gives?

Well, to begin with, some web presence is better than none. Everything you've done on the Internet will show up if someone searches for you. Ideally, there would be a way to have people remove old, irrelevant references. But in the decentralized world of the Web, there's no single repository where you can update your information. Part of the reason for the advice to establish a web site and blog and tweet and friend and circle is that new web activity will push old web activity down in the search results.

So why do we have to worry about being authentic?

Because no one likes a salesman—or, more accurately, someone who appears to be nothing more than a salesman.

But there's something more going on with the Internet than a simple test of your ability to go for more than five minutes without shouting, "Buy my book! Buy my book! Buy my Book!"

The Internet is a slow, not entirely perfect, truth filter. Over time everything on the net is exposed for what it really is. Flashy design and search engine optimization techniques may work for a while, but substance will win out in the long run.

So how do you do authentic?

Authentic is about substance over form: you've got to have content people care about.

Like the boy who cried wolf, it's actually not hard to get someone's attention. What's far more difficult, and hence much more significant, is keeping someone's attention. If there's an author whose books you buy whenever a new one comes out, is it because of the author's antics or because they've consistently given you a good reading experience?

EFFECTIVE AUTHOR PLATFORMS

Livia Blackburn observed that with regard to the critical issue of reaching the audience for which we write books, most author blogs are not very effective.

"At some point, unpublished fiction authors started feeling the pressure to build platforms. The problem is, they forgot all about target audience. Rather than being a means to reach the right readers, blogging became an end in itself.... Fiction writers, being somewhat one-track minded, overwhelmingly decided to blog about writing. ... blogging for writers will not sell your book to the general reading population.... There are thousands of [young adult] and [middle grade] writers (me included), blogging their hearts out to adoring readerships, while ignoring the inconvenient detail that their number of actual teens they're reaching can be counted on one hand." [10]

There is some value in creating an Internet footprint so that when you're shopping your book, agents and editors will have no trouble finding you. But I suspect that many of us are guilty of magical thinking: of believing that if we do all the stuff we're supposed to (without considering whether it's effective) we'll be successful.

If you spend much time in the high-tech industry, you'll run into a Gartner Hype-Cycle chart. [11] The analysts at the Gartner Group use it to assess the relative maturity of various technologies and companies. According to their framework, with any new thing there is an initial spurt of wild expectations ("It will solve all our problems!") followed by an inevitable backlash ("It's not good for anything.") that gives way to a more measured assessment of the innovation's utility and place in the industry.

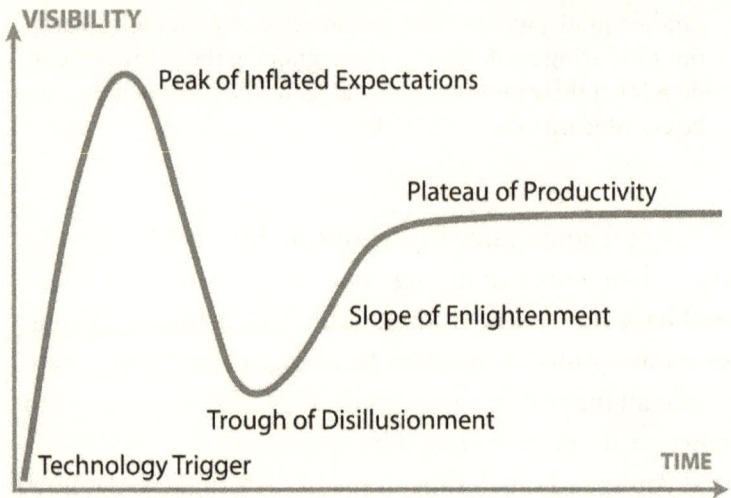

VISIBILITY

Peak of Inflated Expectations

Plateau of Productivity

Slope of Enlightenment

Trough of Disillusionment

Technology Trigger

TIME

Diagram of the Gartner Hype Cycle for new technology.

Author platforms based on social and new media are now past the *Peak of Inflated Expectations*. The early movers—the people well positioned to take advantage of the situation at the beginning of a gold rush—saw astonishing returns on their efforts, giving everyone else inflated expectations. When blogging authors were rare, being online in some fashion was enough. Now every aspiring author has a web site, a blog, a Twitter feed, a Facebook presence, and is in the forefront of the latest social media trends. With so many authors competing for readers' time and attention, why should anyone come to you? The only differentiator that remains under your control is the quality of your content.

That may seem like bad news, but there's an important structural consequence:

THE PLAYING FIELD IS LEVEL

Tracy Hickman has published roughly fifty books and garnered more than six million readers over the course of his career. Yet on his last book tour, only eight people showed up when he signed at the largest sci-fi/fantasy bookstore in San Francisco. He reported that many more people emailed after the fact to say they were sorry they missed him but didn't know he was at the bookstore.

"The playing field is level between you and me," Hickman said. "My readers were used to finding me in the bookstore, but they don't go there anymore."

There's a sea-change underway in publishing. Even Hickman, who has paid his dues many times over, doesn't get a free pass to publishing success. Like the morning sun that burns away the mists, the only thing that truly matters now is finding the people who value your words.

Hickman said:

"What makes you an author? Readers."
"The challenge now is to find your audience, not your publisher."
"The future of publishing is to find, connect with, and maintain your audience."

So, how do you find your audience?

CREATE AN ONLINE CONTEXT FOR DISCOVERY

We talk around notions like building an audience and establishing a reputation. But what does that really mean? Or, more to the point, how can you know if you're doing it well?

The fundamental problem of the Internet is managing abundance. When a quick search returns hundreds of thousands of results, how do you make sense of it? How do you select what is meaningful out of all the background noise?

Meaning depends on context: building a web presence is about creating context; it's how your book will be discovered. This isn't about search engine optimization or other ways of gaming the system. The context (which comes from Latin and means, "with the text,") that matters is the web of relationships, associations, and references that lead ultimately back to your book.

This is why the work itself is the single most important piece of your platform.

THE 90/10 RULE

Even knowing that the aether is awash with conflicting advice, you don't have to read long before you come away with the impression that you must participate in every possible social medium in order to have any hope of success.

But if you do all that, when are you supposed to find time to write the book that you're doing all that to promote?

Your best bet for balancing writing and platform building is the 90/10 rule: spend at least 90% of you time writing and no more than 10% on social media and platform building.

Clearly, "if you build it," they won't simply come. That is, you can't expect to write a novel and then sit back while your audience finds it. But if you haven't written a novel, there won't be anything for your audience to find when you invite them to come.

* * *

The most important professional relationship into which you'll enter is the one with your readers. As the old book distribution system is eclipsed, you have as much access to readers as anyone else. The way to succeed is to use the tried and true techniques, founded on empathy, to create substantive content and deliver it to your readers.

CHAPTER 21.

AT THE SUMMIT

Understanding is often said to be like ascending a mountain. The trail to the peak winds through valleys where ridges obscure the goal. It's only from the summit that you can look back and understand the topographical logic of the trail. As with many things, however, it's also easy to look back and minimize the scope of the journey now that it's over.

You could argue that this book has been nothing more than one long exercise in hammering home the point that professional relationships are not about you. If you get nothing more from this book than that, you're ahead of the pack: it's a lesson most people fail to learn. But I hope you now see the expanding field of possibilities that a constructive approach to professional relationships opens up for you. While Carnegie's first three **Fundamental Techniques in Handling People**, "Don't criticize, condemn, or complain," "Give honest and sincere appreciation," and "Arouse in the other person an eager want," fall under the general heading of *be kind and considerate of others*, there's ample scope for your creativity as you find ways to avoid negativity, express your appreciation, and align your interests with what others want.

Carnegie's **Six Ways to Make People Like You** are really six ways to make yourself more likable:

- Become genuinely interested in other people
- Smile
- Remember that a man's name is to him the sweetest and most important sound in any language
- Be a good listener. Encourage others to talk about themselves
- Talk in the terms of the other man's interest
- Make the other person feel important and do it sincerely

Put another way, the empathy that comes from getting beyond yourself and looking at things from the other person's point of view gives you a tremendous advantage when dealing with people.

Carnegie's final section, **Twelve Ways to Win People to Your Way of Thinking**, shows how it's far better—and far more effective—to entice than compel:

- Avoid arguments
- Show respect for the other person's opinions. Never tell someone they are wrong
- If you're wrong, admit it quickly and emphatically

- Begin in a friendly way
- Start with questions the other person will answer yes to
- Let the other person do the talking
- Let the other person feel the idea is his/hers
- Try honestly to see things from the other person's point of view
- Sympathize with the other person
- Appeal to noble motives
- Dramatize your ideas
- Throw down a challenge and don't talk negative when the person is absent, talk about only positive

The best writing entices. It engenders empathy for and with vivid characters. Above all, it is suffused with kindness and consideration for its readers.

The best professional relationships grow naturally because you present yourself as an enticing partner who is a pleasure to work with because you don't create problems, you solve them.

PART III.

SUSTAINABLE CREATIVITY

CHAPTER 22.

THE SUBSTANCE OF ART

In this book we'll explore creativity and the creative life, using writing to illustrate the broader principles.

Many people who say they want to write really mean they want to have written. That is, many people aspire to be writers because they would like to be in the position of receiving the attention paid to someone who has published a book.

You've probably heard you should write because you have to: don't do it for a living if you can do anything else. That sentiment is best understood as shorthand for the fact that writing is hard work—the kind of hard work only a few people find satisfying. If you find writing to be a joyless chore, perhaps you should do something else.

Writing is a labor of love. Giving birth, the ultimate labor of love, is not at all pleasant but the result is more than worth the effort. But the analogy goes beyond the effort to birth something new because in both cases the new thing takes on a life of its own. The hardest task of all is to relinquish control over your creation.

Art requires real and sustained dedication—much more

than we assume if we only see the end product. The hallmark of mastery is that you make it look easy—as if the work simply flows from your fingertips.

FLOW IN WRITING

You've probably heard about people who say the writing just flowed. It's hard to hear that without taking it to be something mystical or judging yourself to be a lesser writer if you can't make a similar claim.

Wikipedia defines psychological flow this way:

"Flow is the mental state of operation in which a person in an activity is fully immersed in a feeling of energized focus, full involvement, and success in the process of the activity." [1]

There's nothing mystical about flow. Indeed, it is effectively the opposite of mysticism because when you're in a state of psychological flow you're neither awed nor terrified. When you're fully immersed in the process, you find, to the extent that you're even aware of your internal state, that you feel a profound calm.

Flow means you're neither too hot with great ideas, nor too cold bogged down in the details, but just right with ideas and the words to express them coming together at the same time.

Some people argue writing is a purely creative, right-brain activity. There's truth in that claim, particularly for those who see the action and the setting, and hear the voices of their characters. But encoding those ideas in well-chosen words and ordering those words in compelling, grammatically correct sentences is a left-brain activity.

The hardest thing about writing is being sure your reader will get something from the marks on the page similar to what you had in mind when you made them. Unlike speaking with someone, where their expression helps you gauge how well they understand what you're saying, a writer must encode ideas and mental images as words on a page in a medium that can be consumed at another time and place.

Much of the substance of art comes down to mastering the techniques and conventions that usually manage to convey your ideas to your audience. Put more simply, figuring out what you want to say is often easier than figuring out how to say it so that your readers come away thinking about roughly the same thing you were thinking when you wrote.

People who focus on one side of the brain or the other short-change themselves. In my experience, flow is most likely to occur when I've mastered the left-brain mechanics (e.g., proficiency at typing, a command of grammar rules, and a rich vocabulary) and energized the right-brain to focus on the story (and not entertain every distraction that comes along) so both hemispheres are working as a team to produce and encode ideas.

ART AND YOUR INNER CRITIC

Unfortunately, your inner critic also lives in your left-brain and can stifle the wondrous flights of fancy soaring through your right brain. The people who tell you creativity can only flourish if you stay away from the left side of your brain live in fear of their inner critic. Part of the reason art is so often associated with, "recreational chemistry," is because intoxicants are a time-honored way of overcoming your inhibitions.

A self-destructive war between the hemispheres of your brain, however, isn't the only way to produce art. Your inner critic nags at you to keep you safe, not to sabotage your efforts. Jeanette Ingold characterizes our inner critic as, "no-nonsense; it wants to keep you out of trouble; and doesn't want you to make a fool of yourself."

The first step toward embracing your inner critic is to enlist it as your editor—the artistic equivalent of a conscience. Just as real editors help us refine and perfect our work, our internal editor can compliment the work by managing all the details that will make it shine.

There is, of course, a time and a place for everything. You don't, for example, need much help from your internal editor while you're working on your first draft: everything is still fluid and the things that worry your inner editor may get changed before the story finally settles.

So, how do you work with your internal editor?

LIBERATING PROCESSES

Remember, your inner editor is all about the details. The best way to keep your inner editor happy is to keep it busy with detail-oriented tasks like:

- Make a map of where the story takes place.
- Create calendars and time-lines of events critical to the story.
- Keep notes about character decisions.

- Study similar books to see what works and what doesn't.

More generally, having a process helps calm your inner editor. If you work systematically, it's much easier to convince your inner editor you'll come back and correct the details that may be amiss in the early drafts. For example:

- Don't be a binge writer: try to write every day.
- Take advantage of forward momentum. Just keep going forward even if you realize something needs a major change.
- Don't worry about getting the writing perfect. Worry about getting your story on paper. There will be plenty of time with subsequent drafts to polish the text.
- First drafts should be written chronologically.

And when you finish, let your first draft season for a month or so. Read it straight through to the end to get a gut feeling for the pacing. After that first read-through, you can unleash your internal editor, who will get busy and cut out everything that doesn't belong in the story.

If you take a step back, what you're really doing is setting up a cycle of creation and refinement that you'll repeat until the work is finished.

MINDFUL WRITING

Scott Livingston said, "Poetry is intentional brevity."

You have a responsibility as a writer to produce purposeful prose: narratives crafted with intent that give the reader a well-prepared experience. There's no place in writing for pool-hall bravado (i.e., claiming you intended the balls to go where ever they went).

Flow is the state where you're so fully immersed in the process that you stop worrying and simply do. It's a frictionless balance between right-brain vision and left-brain detail.

The synthesis of flow and purpose is mindful writing. Like the Zen practice of mindfulness, which is to, "pay attention in a particular way: on purpose, in the present moment, and non-judgmentally," when you're mindful of your writing, you're both aware and not aware of what you're doing. [2] You see the story and hear the voices of the characters. At the same time you're capturing what you see in specific and intentionally chosen words.

While a perfect, Zen-like union of apparent opposites—in this case the two sides of our brains—in a creative synthesis may seem unobtainable, as you practice mindful writing you'll find the amplitude of the create/refine cycle decreasing as the frequency increases. In other words, you'll become consistently creative and produce higher quality work.

* * *

Our study of creativity and the creative life continues, in chapter two, by clarifying the distinction between an idea and the expression of that idea, and shows how creativity is primarily about the latter. In chapter three, we expand on the notion that creativity is only meaningful in context. Ideas provide creative fuel.

Chapter four explores ways to generate and collect ideas and chapter five looks at how the raw material of a collection of ideas can be organized into a whole greater than the sum of its parts. We turn to a series of observations, inspired by Austin Kleon, on the creative life in chapter six. Sustainable creativity requires discipline. Chapter seven describes simple and creative ways to improve your discipline. In chapter eight we face the uncomfortable truth that creativity is hard work, and look at how you can step up to the challenge. Chapter nine suggests a number of techniques for organizing your affairs in order to clear time and space in which to exercise your creativity. Finally, chapters ten and eleven examine repeatability and the subtle problem of staying creative over the long term.

CHAPTER 23.

EXPRESSION

In order to understand the problem of creativity, consider the problem of mental telepathy. We generally portray telepaths as having access to people's secret inner monologues. But brain scans have only found a general correlation between firing neurons in specific regions and simple activities. While you might be able to use a brain scan to determine when someone is frightened or amorous, there's no way to tell why they feel that way from the seething electrochemical activity in a conscious brain. The practical upshot is that until an idea has been expressed, there's no monologue—not even a finished thought—for a telepath to fish out of the sea of synapses.

When we talk about creativity, we tend to focus on *the idea* because it's the most dramatic part of the story. We conveniently overlook the fact that the idea is the culmination, not the genesis, of the creative process. Even though a spark causes the explosion, it would do nothing more than fizzle without the painstaking and thoroughly unglamorous work of placing and priming the explosives.

Ever since an ad executive published a wildly popular

book on brainstorming in 1953, we've assumed that creativity is a numbers game: the more ideas per hour, the more creativity. But ideas are only the raw material for creativity. Like telepathy, creativity is about the finished thought, not the unorganized jumble of ideas.

PROTECTING IDEAS

Writing can be protected in the United States with a copyright but not with a patent.

What's the difference?

Patents protect ideas. Copyrights protect the expression of ideas.

This means there's nothing to stop you from writing a story about a boy wizard who falls for a sparkly vampire while they're trying to survive as contestants in a blood-sport arena. The fact that other writers have already expressed those ideas in books that achieved commercial success doesn't necessarily stop you from expressing the same ideas—as long as it is a new expression and not plagiarism or a cheap knock-off. What matters, both in the eyes of the law and in the marketplace, is the quality of the expression of the idea.

There's an analogy between copyright law and the ideas that spring up as you imagine the story you'll write. In your enthusiasm for those ideas, you'll be tempted to share. There's nothing as heady as cornering someone to listen while you explain how great the story will be. The ideas are all present and vibrant for you. But great ideas about what could happen in your story are meaningless until you express them in a copyrightable form (i.e., write them down). Put another way, if, like the tree that falls in the forest, no one else can enjoy the idea in its expressed form, then for all practical purposes, it didn't happen.

SELF EXPRESSION

"What is voice?" the new writer asks. "How do I develop one?"

"I know it when I see it," the agent or editor answers. Or they may try to help by recommending books they think have a great voice.

So the new writer absorbs the voice, tries to write something similar, is told their piece has no voice, and comes away feeling increasingly frustrated.

Artists, with their tracing paper, learn by copying. Why can't we?

After all, isn't imitation the sincerest form of flattery?

Ah, but there's the problem: imitation.

Just like high schools that are full of young people trying to find themselves by behaving exactly like all the other young people trying to find themselves, you won't find what's authentically you by imitating someone else.

Writing is, in part, about self-expression—not in the sense of spouting off your opinions, but in the deeper sense of the self you express.

The reason we have trouble with voice is because we've absorbed so many influences and have built up so many assumptions about the nature of writing we've lost touch with our own unique modes of expression.

In narrative, a first person voice should sound like a unique individual.

Third person stories add the voice of the narrator to the chorus of characters.

But voice is much more than characters-with-attitude. Voice is how the narrator chooses to tell the story.

Go back to the primordial camp fires. What set the

storyteller apart from other people when they all knew the story? It was the way he or she told it.

This gets to the heart of your voice as an author:

- What do you include?
- What do you leave out?
- What do you emphasize?
- How do you describe things?

There's an analogy with photography. A thousand people might snap a photo of something but only the photographer produces memorable images. Why? It's because he or she has an eye—an uncommon way of looking at things and framing images.

A photographer's eye, an author's voice; it's about how you express your unique perspective.

How do you find your voice and your unique perspective?

The old-fashioned way: practice.

Read. Write. Repeat.

You may have to write a number of rough drafts before your voice surfaces. Writing every day will help you get past all the influences and assumptions you've internalized.

MASTERY AND CRITICISM

As part of a course in museum studies, we toured a number of museums. The more museums I visited the more I noticed that the explanatory text in exhibits was usually too small. Developing your professional sensibilities can take the fun out of something. Once you understand what it takes to put something together, it's hard to keep from noticing the parts and simply appreciate the whole.

As you become more proficient at your art, you will be tempted to become more critical of others. I went through a phase where I scrutinized new books and in almost every case wondered why they had been released. For example, one book had the phrase "suddenly he slowly ..." To be fair, there were actually very few problems with the books, but I judged them as less polished, in terms of art or craft, than we're told our unpublished work must be if we want agents or editors to consider it.

The siren call of criticism is particularly alluring if you believe you've begun to understand the secret book of rules, the violation of even the smallest of which eliminates your chances for publication. But this is nothing new. The name for second-year students—sophomore—is commonly thought to be a compound of the Greek words for wise and foolish: someone who knows just enough to be dangerous.

Be wary of sophomore mistakes as you travel the path to mastery in your art. Instead of rushing in to criticize with the rest of the fools, take a cue from the wise who have held back. Rather than condemning a book and its publisher see what you can learn by asking questions like, "What was the editorial process?" and, "What led to the decision to go with this book and not another?"

* * *

The essential problem of artistic expression is captured

succinctly in a pair of lines from the chorus to the song **Limelight** by the band Rush:

> … put aside the alienation,
> Get on with the fascination

True creative expression is driven by fascination and thwarted by alienation. Dismissive criticism, an imitative voice, and paranoia about protecting ideas are manifestations of the alienating fear of others mingled with self doubt. Focusing on the tangible expression of your ideas, in your unique voice, enlightened and enlivened by what others have done is the first step toward true creativity.

CHAPTER 24.

CONTEXT

At the first meeting for one of the courses in my masters program, the professor said he hoped to teach us how to read during the coming semester. By this point in graduate school I'd already amassed a substantial collection of books, a degree, and debt—all of which was surely proof I already knew how to read. I was, naturally, a bit put out. But I'd been in school long enough to know one often needs patience when dealing with a new professor.

Each week we read a different book. And each week the professor would begin the discussion by asking, "So how do we get out from under this book?" Over the course of the semester, he showed us that in order to read critically we needed to understand the context—literally, what came with the text. He helped us explore the context by asking questions like:

- Who is the author?
- Where were they?

- When did they write?
- What else was happening when they wrote?

For instance, we read a book about the anti-abolition riots during 1830-1840 that was written during the civil-rights riots of the late 1960s and early 1970s.

Coincidence?

Art doesn't exist in a vacuum. There is no absolute art that will be universally recognized as such. The ancient art that we lovingly unearth and preserve was once discarded and forgotten. Modern masterpieces and cultural treasures would simply be part of the rubbish if the world were destroyed.

As artists and writers, we need to understand both the internal and external contexts. Internal context includes everything from a sensible plot to a sensible back story and a sufficiently fleshed-out setting. External context includes the world and market into which the work is introduced, the influences and common cultural associations, and all the things to which the author may have been responding when they produced the work.

INTERNAL CONTEXT: PARTS AND WHOLES

Optical illusions are fun because of the way they jump from one thing to another as you look at them. Being able to see things—particularly the situations in which you find yourself—in more than one way is essential to creativity.

One of the interesting aspects of working with computers is the number of orders of magnitude you need to comprehend. You can work with processes that take anywhere from nanoseconds to months or years to complete. You need the mental agility to move across those time scales, seeing the parts at one scale as the wholes at the next, in order to build robust computing systems.

Creating an effective internal context is, first and foremost, about balance. People working with systems must always be on their guard against the subtle trap of optimizing a component at the expense of a system. In a computing system, premature optimization is usually a waste of time because you can't be certain how a component affects overall performance until the system is complete. With writing you might spend time perfecting a scene only to find later that it doesn't advance the story and must be cut.

At a deeper level, internal context is about rhyme and reason. What is the role of the parts in the context of the larger system? Why, in the case of this particular story, are things the way they are? It's often said the best stories are surprising yet inevitable. Internal context creates both the surprise and the inevitability.

But how do you do it?

THE FIVE WHYS

A basic part of engineering discipline is to determine root causes. If, for example, defective items start to flow down an assembly line, it's much more efficient to find and correct the cause of the defect upstream than to expend extra energy to compensate for it downstream. You can't engineer a real solution if you don't know what's actually happening.

Story arises from conflicting forces and motivations. If those forces and motivations are definitional (e.g., the villain is simply evil) the story will feel more contrived than a story in which the forces and motivations flow naturally from root causes.

So, how can you get to the root causes as either a writer or an engineer?

One powerful method is the *Five Whys*. While it sounds like an exercise in being an annoying child, the essence of the method is to ask, "Why?" at least five times:

1. Why is a particular character the villain? *Because he's evil.*
2. Why is he evil? *Because he hates people.*
3. Why does he hate people? *Because he's never known anyone who didn't let him down, beginning with his parents.*
4. Why did his parents let him down? *Because they ignored him.*
5. Why did they ignore him? *Because they were too busy working with the League of Do-Gooders.*

This simplistic example illustrates the method of digging deeper with the *Five Whys*: we've gone from a bland, definitional villain to one that has a bit of depth—though not nearly enough yet to be a compelling antagonist. Which brings us to a second point about the method: it's something you must use repeatedly to really understand the situation. In our example, we should use the *Five Whys* to explore how the villain came to power, what his plans are, and so on.

MEETING THE MARKET

People tend to see the world in dichotomies. Psychologists tell us that the tendency toward dualisms, like black and white or good and bad, comes from the fact that our brains are wired to distinguish between me and not me. There are many cases where reducing the complex world to one of two cases serves us well. But living in a complex society, we're often better served by an approach that eschews the extremes as being either too hot or too cold and focuses instead on the region in the middle that's just right.

So what does this have to do with your integrity as a creative person?

There are two inaccurate caricatures of writers which have analogs in all creative endeavors: the hack that panders to the market and the artist whose work must be good because it is obscure and impenetrable. The goal of every high quality writer should be to follow Baby Bear's example and produce books that are just right. In other words, you need to meet the market halfway with your creativity.

Everything happens in context. Take your favorite genius (say Mozart or Einstein) out of context (i.e., drop them in the middle of the jungle) and they're no longer a genius (or, more accurately, none of their new acquaintances care).

It actually takes more creativity to do something fresh within a well defined context than to have a field day with a blank slate. You can write a book with integrity if you take contexts, conventions, and expectations, and add your love, personality, and creativity to produce a new synthesis.

CHAPTER 25.

THE ART OF COLLECTING IDEAS

I once heard a rabbi say, "You know the story of the Burning Bush and how Moses turned aside to see it. I like to believe that Moses wasn't the first to see the burning bush, but that he was the first to turn aside."

While taking care not to conflate artists and prophets, one of the simplest yet most effective ways to collect ideas is being willing to turn aside and see something—even something incredibly ordinary—in a new light or with new eyes.

As we morph from children into adults, we move from a world of concrete and specific things into a world of abstractions and classes. The process is innocent enough. When a child points at the feathered creature hopping across the lawn and asks, "What is that?" they want to know about the specific one in front of them. When we answer, "Oh, that's a robin," we give the child a word for a class of birds, of which the specific one they see is simply a representative. In time, we stop seeing the particular bird and see instead an instance of a robin.

What is the technique for seeing something special where others don't?

Like the child, ask, "What is that one? How did that one come to be here and now?"

Human language is powerful because of its abstractions, generalizations, and indirections. Most people use that power for their own purposes without realizing the degree to which they are, in turn, controlled or at least constrained by it. Writers, who regularly wrestle words to make meaning, are among the best equipped to get out from under the oppression of abstractions and turn aside, like Moses, to see what others pass by.

CHARACTER NAMES

Finding names for our characters is a good example of the general habit of wondering how the things you notice came to be.

The pattern is simple:

- Find interesting names
- Play with the implications of the names.

Interesting names appear all the time in the written and spoken environment. I once noticed, "glycol ester of wood rosin," among the list of ingredients in a bottled drink. Instead of fretting about the obscure food additives I'd just ingested, I wondered how Esther Glycol, the Regency-era daughter of an impoverished vicar, came to be mistress of the estate of Woodrosin. (You didn't know you could get all of that from an FDA-mandated list of ingredients, did you?)

If you need to find names more quickly, you can play the phone book game: open to a random page and drop your finger to select a given name or a surname. On one occasion, when I needed a set of modern, ethnically diverse names, I collected all the surnames and given names from the credits of a recent movie and then randomly recombined them.

If you know a programming language, it's a relatively simple matter to randomly combine names from two or more lists. If the set of surnames isn't too large, you'll get multiple names with the same surname and naturally wonder how they are related. Not only will you have names, you'll have partial genealogies, and perhaps some ideas about family histories as well.

I've also used random generators to assemble names from syllable lists for fantastic or alien characters. One nice side effect of this approach is that the names sound like they came from the same culture because they follow the same pattern.

The important thing is to generate a number of names and then choose the ones that speak to you. Play with the names that are most evocative and see what else springs to mind. [3]

REBUTTAL THEORY

Shannon Hale said her approach to retelling fairy tales was motivated by the question, "What's bugging me about this story?"

I started thinking seriously about this question after reading several books that bugged me so much I had to make a rebuttal. It's not that I had problems with the books themselves as much as some of the ideas in the stories.

Two interesting things happened as I thought about the ideas that bugged me in each story and the ways in which I might handle them differently:

1. I was drawn into the process of thinking through each idea and uncovered a host of interesting new ideas.
2. The different lines of inquiry came together as a fascinating new story molecule.

Hale's question, "What's bugging me about this story?" is a powerful idea generator if you follow it with a second question: "How would I do it differently?"

There's another important consequence: if you work through the ideas until you can clearly express what bothers you about the story and how you would handle it differently, you'll find you have something to add to the conversation.

SWITCH THINGS UP

Like the old beer commercial where people argued whether the best thing about the brew was that it, "tastes great," or that it's, "less filling," writers often argue whether it's better to outline before you write or to make it up as you go along. The partisans call themselves, "plotters," and, "pantsers," (as in, seat-of-the-pants) respectively.

We'd be further ahead to view plotting and pantsing, not as defining our nature but as techniques in our toolbox we use—like an illustrator may use pastels for one picture and oils for another—when appropriate.

In a study, described in a post titled, *Unusual Thinking Styles Increase Creativity*, people who solved problems, "using systematic patterns of thought," and people who solved problems, "by setting the[ir] mind[s] free to explore associations," were asked to change their problem-solving style. [4] The researchers wondered if people's creativity could be increased by encouraging them to use the pattern of thinking that was most unusual to them. So, those people who naturally preferred to approach creative problems rationally were asked to think intuitively. And the intuitive group was asked to think rationally for a change. Participants were given a real-world problem to solve: helping a local business expand. The results, which were evaluated by managers from the company involved, supported the hypothesis: people were more creative when they used the thinking style that was most unusual for them.

One of the reasons this may work is that consciously adopting a different strategy means your mind can't go down the same well-travelled paths. We all have habitual ways of approaching problems that tend to produce the same kinds of results. The parallel should be clear: plotters prefer to write rationally; pantsers prefer to write intuitively. You likely feel more comfortable in one mode or the other. But if your deeper goal is to write creatively you would do well to switch up your style from time to time.

DON'T BE SATISFIED WITH YOUR FIRST IDEA

Implicit in the advice to not be satisfied with your first idea is the assumption that you started with a good idea.

Being certain you have a good idea is much harder than recognizing when your idea falls short of good.

The first litmus test for a poor idea is simple: is it your first idea?

In the game show **Family Feud**, the challenge wasn't to come up with the correct answer but to guess the answers given by the hundred people surveyed. Of the four or five hidden answers, the top one or two usually accounted for more than half the responses. That is, the first answer that came to mind for the contestant likely came to mind for every second or third person taking the survey.

"Novel," means new. If you go with your first idea, you stand a good chance of not having something novel and instead going down a well-worn path. If you want to be a novelist, you must internalize Monty Python's catch phrase, "And now for something completely different."

But this isn't novelty simply for novelty's sake. The deeper challenge is to take the raw concept and make it your own.

Chances are, your first idea really isn't your idea. (Why, after all, did so many of the people surveyed for the game show come up with the same answer?) It's simply the first association that bubbled up into your consciousness. The first association is likely the strongest, having been reinforced by external influences. To make the idea your own, you need to let it steep in your unique soup of mental associations until it morphs into something that's unmistakably you.

THE HALLMARKS OF A GOOD IDEA

It seems only proper, after encouraging you to distrust your first idea, that we should look into the question of how you know you have a good idea.

Of course, it's not possible to be certain you have a good idea until you test it on others. If it were, we'd have institutions, modeled on drug companies, devoted to finding and exploiting as many good ideas as possible. So the good news is that no one has a monopoly on good ideas. The bad news is that the best we can do is find heuristics to help us sort the good ideas from the bad.

One of the best heuristics I've found is that good ideas have a longer shelf life or more staying power than mediocre ideas. You may be on to something if an idea keeps coming back to you, whereas bad ideas are, actually, forgettable.

But, *comes back to you* means something more than simply remembering the idea. A good idea should give you an electric shimmer along your spine each time you savor it.

DON'T STOP WITH ONE GOOD IDEA

John Lasseter, of Pixar, tells his animators, "Never come up with just one idea."

Here's how John explains it:

"Regardless of whether you want to write a book, design a piece of furniture or make an animated movie: At the beginning, don't start with just one idea – it should be three…. The problem with creative people is that they often focus their whole attention on one idea. So, right at the beginning of a project, you unnecessarily limit your options. Every creative person should try that out. You will be surprised how this requirement suddenly forces you to think about things you hadn't even considered before. Through this detachment, you suddenly gain new perspectives. And believe me, there are always three good ideas. At least." [5]

The first key here, and it bears repeating, is, "this requirement suddenly forces you to think about things you hadn't even considered before." There are a lot of people out there having good ideas. If you stop with your first good idea, chances are very good that someone has already thought of it. But with each additional good idea you bring to the table, the chance of someone else thinking of the exact same set of ideas drops dramatically.

The second key is the perspective you gain through detachment. That is, if you have more than one good idea then you've got a fall-back if one of the ideas proves less good than you thought. More importantly, you can compare and contrast the ideas and get a better sense of their relative merit.

* * *

I don't notice the makes and models of vehicles on the road unless I'm shopping for a car. Each time I've set out to purchase an automobile, I've had the peculiar experience of learning about a new model and then seeing it everywhere. The cars, of course, were there all along but I didn't see them until I began to pay attention.

In the same way, there are, like butterflies, more ideas out there than you can possibly collect or use in a lifetime. The real problem is how to use them well.

CHAPTER 26.

THE SCIENCE OF USING IDEAS

Brandon Sanderson said, "Writers train themselves to notice interesting things, wonder about them, and construct novels to answer their own questions."

The difference between creative people and others is not in the quantity or quality of ideas but in what they do with the ideas after they come: creative people hang on to ideas and bounce them off of each other until they start to stick together. Unusual juxtapositions and stimulating associations live at the core of creativity. Once enough idea atoms start to stick together, they form the nucleus around which a story can crystallize.

Put differently, because of the way books are marketed (publishers love nothing better than an evocative word or phrase that seems to capture the essence of the book), it's easy to assume that writers are home-free once they have a clever concept. Nothing could be further from the truth. The art of the novel is what you do with that clever concept to keep it interesting across hundreds of pages. A novel is actually the sum of tens of thousands of ideas all working together to create the pattern of a story that, from a distance, looks like a single clever concept.

PRIMING YOUR CREATIVITY

People assume writers enjoy a generous endowment of creativity. Creativity is defined (at dictionary.com) as, "the ability to transcend traditional ideas, rules, patterns, relationships, or the like, and to create meaningful new ideas."

Many people treat that ability as something innate and quasi-mystical. The problem with believing ideas spring forth from a fount of creativity is that if you don't have a great idea handy the well may have run dry and you're stuck until something happens to get your creativity flowing again.

Author John Brown says the secret to the creative process is:

Ask questions and come up with answers.

A bit anti-climactic?

Perhaps I should clarify: a creative person doesn't settle for one answer to each question. If you stop after the first answer, you've done nothing more than identify a common idea. Before you choose an answer, you want to come up with as many varied solutions, particularly unexpected solutions, as you can. Given a large enough pool of candidate ideas, it's much easier to find meaningful new ones.

So how do you prime the creative pump?

Pay attention. Notice things, particularly the things

that strike you as interesting or intriguing. John suggests you collect things that give you a little, "zing," when you hear or read about them.

And what do you do when you've collected enough ideas?

STORY MOLECULES

When people ask where the ideas in a novel came from, they generally assume that the book was produced through an alchemical process that harnesses mystic forces to transmute the base metals of common ideas into the gold of a finished story. The truth, like the transmutation of alchemy into the cold, hard science of chemistry is more prosaic. Like chemistry, which produces complex and beautiful molecular structures through a series of processes, the final form of the story molecule in a novel is the result not of mystic transmutations but processes that anyone who is patient and persistent can master.

So, how do you build a story molecule?

Begin with the basic creative process: ask questions and then generate lots of answers so that you can find the most interesting associations. Often, the best associations will be between something common and something, which in the context of the first idea, is surprising.

Stick those ideas together and then add others that bring additional surprises to the mix.

STRENGTH THROUGH ASSOCIATION

You've likely heard the spiritual, Dem Bones, and know that the toe bone's connected to the foot bone, and the foot bone's connected to the ankle bone, and so on. It's both an anatomy lesson, of sorts, and reference to the Biblical prophet Ezekiel's vision of a valley of dry bones.

In the vision, Ezekiel prophesied, as commanded, to the bones and they came together, bone to bone, and sinews and flesh until, "an exceeding great army," stood before him. Without worrying about the religious significance of the vision, we can appreciate the structural significance: by themselves, the bones are dry and impotent but in proper association with flesh and sinew they become a terrible strength and beauty that is greater than the sum of its parts.

One of the primary functions of the mass of interconnected neurons inside our skulls is to make associations.

Story molecules are a constellation of ideas, working together, to sustain a long-form narrative. Associations are what bind those ideas together.

Think of it this way: if ideas are points, associations are the lines joining those points. Two points can be joined with one line. With three points, each can be connected to the other two with three lines. Four points have six lines of pair-wise associations, five points have ten, and six points have fifteen. Each time you add one more idea, the number of possible connections jumps. It doesn't take many ideas before you have a rich web of associations between them.

Another way to look at it is that associating two ideas is a simple way to create a whole (the associated ideas) greater than the sum of the parts (the ideas in isolation).

Let's play a game: we'll start with one object, a gun, and associate it by proximity (i.e., placing it next to) another:

- What comes to mind if we place our gun next to a shot of whiskey?

- Now, what comes to mind if we place our gun next to a pair of baby shoes?

Associations become even more powerful if we link ideas into a chain. There was a fascinating series on PBS called **Connections**, in which host James Burke showed how an event or innovation in the past traced, "through a series of seemingly unrelated connections to a fundamental and essential aspect of the modern world." [6]

The associations in your stories need not be so profound, but you can use the same principle, particularly when brainstorming, to turn common-place ideas into something special.

WORKING WITH GREAT IDEAS

So, what do you do when you have a story molecule made up of great idea atoms in intriguing relationships?

Like any good evil genius, you turn to science!

More to the point, you turn to the history of science. Thomas Khun, a physicist who also studied the history of science, published **The Structure of Scientific Revolutions** in 1962. In that book, Kuhn challenged the notion that science was steadily progressive and argued it was, instead, episodic. [7]

Kuhn's key ideas are the alternating phases of revolutionary and normal science that make up an episode.

Revolutionary science is the time when a breakthrough

throws the field wide open. Like settlers pouring into new territory, scientists rush from one discovery to the next as they map out the new landscape of possibilities.

Once the early leaders in the revolution have discovered the extent of the breakthrough, the discipline settles back into normal science mode. Normal science is far less glamorous than revolutionary science because it's about the careful work of confirming the initial findings and filling in the details.

"That's nice for historians and scientists," you might say, "but what does it have to do with writing, or creativity in general?"

A great idea is like the breakthrough that triggers a period of revolutionary science. But that's only the beginning of the job. In order to develop a novel-length story, you must do the literary equivalent of the work of normal science.

Let's say you've just had an epiphany: the world will end when pigs actually start to fly—it's the Flying Pig Apocalypse! Tingling with excitement, you sit down to write … and immediately run into questions: how do they fly? Levitation? Wings that grow because a mad scientist wanted bacon-flavored Buffalo wings? Lighter-than air gas bladders? Do they flock or are they loners? Do they cause the apocalypse by flying, or is the fact that they take flight a sign of the impending apocalypse? There's clearly a great deal more work to do before the flying pigs and their apocalypse are ready to burst upon book stores.

Like science, which we tend to think of only in terms of revolutionary breakthroughs, creativity is more about the normal work of thinking carefully through the great idea than the revolutionary work of having the idea in the first place.

CHAPTER 27.

THE CREATIVE LIFE

On March 30, 2011, Austin Kleon posted a presentation, titled, *How to Steal Like an Artist (and 9 Other Things Nobody Told Me)* [8], of the ten things he's come to understand about living a creative life. I was so impressed I immediately took Kleon's advice and stole his presentation—like an artist.

This chapter is a riff on Kleon's ten points.

ONE: STEAL LIKE AN ARTIST

Kleon's first piece of advice was motivated by his honest answer to the inevitable where-do-you-get-your-ideas question: he said, "I steal them."

Before your ethical early-warning system goes into a tizzy, remember that copyright protects the expression, not the idea. J.K. Rowling's lawyers can't do anything to stop you if you want to tell a story about a boy at a boarding school for wizards as long as it is your own expression of that idea.

"NOTHING IS ORIGINAL"

With between six and seven billion minds on the planet right now, what, statistically, is the chance that no one else has ever had an idea similar to yours?

Add the constraints of archetypes, and only a handful of fundamentally different stories, and you don't have much scope for something unique. (This, by the way, is why agents reject quickly if you claim there's nothing on the market like your manuscript.)

It would be easy to decide it's not worth trying because it has already been done when you hear that nothing is original. But Kleon says the idea gives him hope: instead of wandering in the desert, spending a lifetime searching for an original idea, you can drink deeply from the same well everyone else uses. What matters is not the idea, but how you use it.

"YOU ARE THE SUM OF YOUR INFLUENCES"

Consider a brain grown in a vat. How many encyclopedias would you need to give it if you wanted it to appreciate your novel? In fact, without first downloading Wikipedia, what are the chances that you and the brain would have enough common points of reference to be able to communicate at all?

We exist, physically, socially, and mentally, in a vast web of shared ideas. Our explicit communication is only the visible part of an iceberg of references and associations.

That last sentence, for example, works only if you know that icebergs are mountains of ice floating in the ocean with only about 10% of their mass visible above the surface. Imagine how exhausting communication would be if we had to spell out every reference, allusion, and association.

STEALING LIKE AN ARTIST

What does this mean for those of us who aspire to unique expressions?

An artist *steals* by becoming a conceptual omnivore, selecting and saving the ideas that resonate most strongly in a mental stock pot where their essences can commingle: the richer your broth of influences, the better your chances for making a unique association, or hitting upon a twist that is both surprising and inevitable.

TWO: DON'T WAIT UNTIL YOU KNOW WHO YOU ARE TO MAKE THINGS

There's an old wisecrack that, in this age of iPods, is fading into disuse: ask a teenager what instrument they play and they'll say, "The stereo."

For much of human history, the only music you had was the music you made yourself. Prior to the era of recorded music, for example, refined young women were expected to entertain with their playing and singing. Now it seems more common for people to not even bother to learn an instrument because even with a lot of effort they still don't sound as good as the $0.99 download.

We're often told—and often believe—we can't be truly creative until we know who we are. Kleon argues that the best way to learn who you are is to make things. It's a powerful insight.

But the common advice also has a point: we're not going to be able to add anything new to the conversation until we have some idea of who we are, what we know, and what we want to say.

The difference between the two is that the common advice refers to the product while Kleon is talking about process.

It takes time and effort—including some soul searching to figure out what you have to contribute—before people will sit up and take notice when you play anything other than the stereo. But you'll never master the instrument if you only practice scales and postpone making music until you think you're good enough.

If you've focused on short stories and writing exercises because you don't think you're good enough to write your novel, you're on the path of self-fulfilling prophesy. Granted, short stories are a better way to prepare to write a novel than playing video games. But the best way to prepare to write a novel is to write a novel.

Kleon also encourages us to play and to, "Fake it till you make it." Children don't wait until they're good at something before they try it and it doesn't matter if they fail. We spend most of our time as adults either dealing with the consequences of failure or working to avoid it. But an all-or-nothing approach—we must succeed: failure is not an option—stunts our creative life, confining it to the tiny areas where we know we can succeed.

What, then, is the synthesis between the caution of common wisdom and Kleon's liberating advice? Simply this: don't expect to write a bestseller the first time you put pen to paper and don't let that knowledge stop you from trying.

THREE: WRITE THE BOOK YOU WANT TO READ

Kleon's third suggestion sounds simply like a variation on the common writing advice to not chase trends.

Why is that advice so common? Or, more to the point, why do we need to repeat it so often?

It all comes down to return on investment.

A novel requires a substantial investment of time and energy. As relatively rational economic actors, we all would like some assurance we'll receive a return on that investment at least equal to our opportunity costs. (Or, in simpler terms, we'd love to know if we're wasting our time.)

Writing to a trend is seductive because we can point to a proven market.

But consider this: if through means fair or foul you acquired a time machine just long enough to pop back to, say, 1995 and tell your younger self that a story about an eleven-year-old boy going off to a boarding school for wizards was a sure thing, how likely is it that you would have a castle in Scotland now?

Remember, it's not the idea but the execution that matters.

So we're back to square one: how do you know that your book will be worth the effort?

Kleon's answer is to write what you like; to produce the book you would read if it were available.

No one really knows what's going to work. If they did, the major corporations that own the big publishers would manufacture all the best-sellers and shut us would-be scribblers out of the market.

You might sigh, nod, and say, "I suppose if I write the book I want, then at least one person will like it."

That's true in a minimal sense, but Kleon's advice captures something more powerful and empowering: if you like it—if the story really speaks to you—there's a very good chance others will like it too.

FOUR: USE YOUR HANDS

If you've been writing for any length of time, there's advice you've probably heard so often that your partner sometimes has to wake you in the middle of the night and tell you to stop mumbling, "Show don't tell," in your sleep. A corollary to that writerly axiom is that we should engage all our reader's senses when showing. So it's deeply ironic that we scribblers often do our work watching screens as we type on keyboards, using as few of our senses and as little of our body as possible.

Kleon calls for the opposite: to engage the work with as much of your body and as many of your senses as possible.

When we talk about being fully engaged, we're usually referring to people's attention. But consider the times when you've been fully engaged in a physical activity. Perhaps it was the bottom of the ninth, or in the morning cool of a garden, or dancing with a certain someone. In those moments, do you remember thinking about where to put your feet and what you had to do next, or did one movement flow into another?

In the psychological state of flow—a conceptual analog to superconductivity—the distinction between you and the work blurs and everything seems to come together almost effortlessly. Flow is more common when you're physically engaged in an activity. It springs from the joy of feeling fully alive.

I have a three-year-old nephew whose barely contained glee with all the things he can (or imagines he can) do drives him to fling himself bodily into every bed, cushion, or pile of leaves. And if he suffers a bump or bruise, he cries with the same passion until it's time, a few minutes later, to leap into the next adventure.

On a quieter note, I have, for many years, supplied my family with flour tortillas. It's difficult to reduce the experience of mixing, kneading, forming, rolling, and cooking tortillas to words. I have to use my hands to explain how and why I shape a round of dough before I roll it out. Sometimes, it's as though the day's frustrations melt out of my arms as I knead the dough. Sometimes, it's like making mud pies when I was as buoyant as my nephew. Over the years, I suspect I've saved a significant amount on therapy while producing something warm and tasty to share with those near and dear.

One of the subtly sad things about growing up is internalizing all the ways in which we must restrain ourselves. So, one of the best and simplest ways to tap into our creativity is to channel your inner three-year-old and get dirty with joyous abandon.

FIVE: SIDE PROJECTS AND HOBBIES ARE IMPORTANT

In a perfect world, Kleon's fifth point shouldn't need saying. The world in which we live, however, is one most of us would not mistake for perfect. Among the catalog of ills that beset North Americans is that we are immersed in a culture which values long hard work over leisure.

Economic metrics show U.S. workforce productivity growing year after year as we do more with less, cover job functions for people who have been let go and not replaced, and desperately try to realize the myth of multitasking. We even take a perverse sort of pride in getting roughly half as much vacation time as our European counterparts.

An interesting side-effect is that we work just as hard at play as we do at work. If you believe the soft drink adds, you're not really recreating unless you're careening down a mountain on a snow board, mountain bike, or para-glider. We've reduced play to excitement and entertainment by squeezing out time-wasters like concentration and contemplation.

Kleon argues you need to balance your directed activities with non-directed activities (i.e., play) because it is the side projects that often turn into your best work.

Hard work has its place, so long as we don't lose sight of the magic that makes it all meaningful.

There's truth to the cliché about refilling the well. Kleon says, "It's also important to have a hobby. Something that's just for you."

Make time and space where you can play the kinds of quiet games that nourish your creativity.

SIX: DO GOOD WORK THEN PUT IT WHERE PEOPLE CAN SEE IT

One of the unavoidable facts of the creative life—no matter how much we want to believe our art is pure and unsullied by the opinions of others—is that we need an audience: we need to believe there is someone else out there, perhaps not even born yet, who will respond to our work.

Audiences, however, are much harder to come by than you might think. The vast majority of people in the world neither know nor care about you. And of the tiny fraction of humanity who are aware of your existence, most of them are busy with other things.

What, then, can you do to build an audience?

Kleon's answer is, "Do good work and put it where people can see it."

In other words, the only way to build an audience is to provide something to which they're willing to pay attention.

So why, as a creative person, do you share?

VALIDATION

The word, "validation," carries connotations of dependence, but at a certain, fundamental level we need the reassurance that others will respond favorably and that we are, in fact, not crazy.

EXPOSURE

One of the simple, yet powerful metaphors in the **New Testament** is that of a lit candle hid under a basket. It's even more significant if you remember that the metaphor comes from a time when candles weren't cheap or plentiful enough to be squandered on birthday cakes.

A truism of publishing is that the one way to guarantee you'll never get published is to never submit.

FASCINATION

But the best reason to share is because we find something fascinating.

When people ask Kleon the secret to attracting attention on the Internet, his answer is, "Step 1: Wonder at something; Step 2: Invite others to wonder with you."

SEVEN: GEOGRAPHY IS NO LONGER OUR MASTER

There was a time when I was related to nearly half of a small town in south-western Utah. Visiting there as a child, I felt, like Luke Skywalker says of Tatooine, that I'd come to one of the places farthest from the bright center of the galaxy (except there was so little light pollution that the Milky Way blazed in its starry band across the summer nights and it was actually easier to see the bright center of the galaxy there than from other, more civilized places). Now, thanks to telecommunications and significantly improved roads and freeways, that corner of Utah is practically a bedroom community for Las Vegas.

We live—at least in the developed world—in an age of pervasive interconnectivity.

- Distance no longer prevents you from seeing the great works (though there is something ineffable about seeing a thing in its actual setting).

- The accident of location no longer dictates whether or not you may associate with other creative people.

- The tyranny of space no longer prevents you from studying with the masters.

- The confines of your current community no longer keep you from finding the audience who responds most strongly to your work.

In short your latitude and longitude no longer excuse you from your calling to live the creative life.

EIGHT: BE NICE

At one level, it should be obvious that we ought to be kind to the people around us, giving them the benefit of the doubt until they prove otherwise. At another, we need to be reminded because there seems to be no shortage of examples of people getting ahead by behaving badly and taking advantage of others.

As we move forward into the brave, new world where Internet-enabled information streams insinuate themselves into every aspect of our lives, one of the many fading distinctions is the one between cities and small towns. I've lived in both and they have advantages and disadvantages. Small towns are warm and welcoming because everyone knows you, but they can be stifling because everyone knows you. Cities are cold and menacing because no one knows you, but they can also be full of possibilities because no one knows you.

We're moving beyond the time when you could reinvent yourself simply by moving somewhere else and jettisoning your social baggage, and back into a time when, regardless of where you go, everyone knows who you are.

Kleon said:

"... if you talk about someone on the Internet, they will find out. Everybody has a Google alert on their name. The best way to vanquish your enemies on the Internet? Ignore them. The best way to make friends on the Internet? Say nice things about them."

What this means more generally is that as a creative person, you'll always come out ahead by enticing your audience instead of compelling them. Give them a better reason to come to you than your enemy. And sometimes, particularly in terms of professional relationships, that better reason can be as simple as the fact that you are a pleasant person.

NINE: BE BORING. IT'S THE ONLY WAY TO GET WORK DONE.

It's not much of a confession to say I have no patience for the breathless, glitzy Hollywood gossip shows. They're simply an endless parade of celebrities behaving badly. The only reason those programs are worth a mention is that the people they feature are usually too busy being famous to produce anything resembling art.

There's a romantic notion that artists are tortured souls who straddle the boundaries of polite society, finding temporary solace in an excess of wine, women, and song.

The reality is very different.

"The thing is," Kleon said, "art takes a lot of energy to make. You don't have that energy if you waste it on other stuff."

As with everything, there are, of course, outliers, but as usual the exceptions prove the rule: riotous and dissipative living really gets in the way of working on your art.

I'm sure you've had times when you were on fire with creativity. But if you're like me, the flames die down as soon as you start bumping into impediments, running afoul of inertia, and dissipating energy through friction. What I've realized is that those moments are the creative equivalent of afterburners—the speed is exhilarating, but it quickly uses up your fuel.

Art, as a way of life, is a long game. You win, eventually, if you have the staying power to keep showing up. Which means that, like the distance runner, you must pace yourself. And the unfortunate truth is that, like the distance runner, what you spend most of your time doing is going to look boring to outsiders.

There's another important part of being boring: your regular and orderly habits are critical to creating the time and space where creativity can flourish. This is why, for example, one of the most common suggestions for new writers is that they should find a way to write every day, preferably at the same time.

You'll have to decide which particular regular and orderly habits work best for you. But you'd be well-advised to think in those terms if you want to get something done.

TEN: CREATIVITY IS SUBTRACTION

Many people believe that if some is good, more is better.

In truth, less is more: an uncluttered context highlights the creative work—why do you think art galleries have big blank walls?

Think about the creativity of subtraction.

- Sculpture is clearly the art of subtracting the extra material hiding the finished form.
- Music is the art of sounding only a few (usually) consonant tones out of all possible noises at any given time.
- Film is fundamentally about selecting only those images that contribute to the story.
- The best writing conveys powerful images, emotions, and ideas with a few, well-chosen words.

In all these cases, the artist creates a model that emphasizes some aspect of reality while minimizing (or ignoring) the rest of the complex world in which we exist. It is through selective focus that we create meaning.

If the subtractive principle of art is still not clear, then think of a Zen garden where a single stone and a bit of raked sand convey oceans of meaning.

* * *

In this chapter we've explored themes including be genuine, positive, and pleasant; be disciplined; and be confident. But the notion that best sums up Kleon's perspective on the creative life is humility.

Now many people, particularly in a world that lionizes out-of-control celebrities, philandering sports stars, and ruthless captains of industry, think of humility as more of a character flaw than a virtue. Real humility, however, is about perspective not abasement. While it's true that we're put in our place when we realize we're only a small part of the world, the other side of the proverbial coin is the realization we are a part of the world and have a place in it.

So, what is the essence of humility in creativity?

As Kleon says:

Step 1: Wonder at something.
Step 2: Invite others to wonder with you.

CHAPTER 28.

CREATIVE DISCIPLINE

Discipline is a scary word for most people. Perhaps it has something to do with the annual custom of making resolutions when we have to get a new calendar and our inevitable confession, a few weeks or months later, that we failed to keep those resolutions because of a lack of discipline.

The word *discipline* comes from the same root as the word *disciple*, which means a student or follower. To follow the discipline of a mystic or teacher means conforming to an often complex set of practices. From that comes the general sense that only the strictest and most dedicated people are truly disciplined. So we associate discipline with regimentation, the mortal enemy of creativity.

But if we strip away the formalities, discipline is nothing more than being consistent. Mastering any non-trivial art requires consistent effort: it's not about regimentation, it's about focus.

So how do we reconcile discipline with the creative freedom to break conventions and explore new territory?

LITTLE SYSTEMS

I learned about little systems from Jim McCarthy's **Dynamics of Software Development**, [9] where he talked about a pair of coffee shops in Seattle (this was before Starbucks was synonymous with coffee shops—sometime in the late Cretaceous). At one shop, the coffee was consistently excellent. In the other, it was hit-or-miss. The shops were the same in all material aspects: facilities, locations, offerings, staff, and clients. The only difference was that in the consistently good shop all the pots had a line etched about half-an-inch from the bottom.

That little line—and the standing rule that if the level of the coffee fell below the line the staff was to brew a new pot—made all the difference. When things got busy in the hit-or-miss shop the staff wouldn't notice they were out until they drained a pot. Then customers had to wait until the staff brewed a new pot. If there were too many people in line, the staff sometimes succumbed to the temptation to pull the pot before the coffee was ready.

The coffee pot system is about as simple as they come: one mark and one rule. If I hadn't labeled it as a, "little system," you likely would have barely noticed it if you worked in that shop. The key point is that little systems blend into the background and become nothing more than, "the way we do things here." If the system requires enough ceremony that you notice, it's too big.

You probably already use a number of little systems but don't think of them as such. The rest of this chapter goes through some examples of little systems to help jump-start your thinking about ways to apply this subtle but powerful idea as you make time and space for your creative endeavors.

CHECK LISTS

A check list is a great example of a little system because it simplifies a process by reducing it to a series of small steps or checks.

The magic is not in the list, but the steps.

Consider a list like this:

- Find site for evil lair
- Recruit minions
- Invent doomsday device
- Take over world

The steps in a check list need to be small and concrete, unlike the list above. Ideally, the steps shouldn't require much thought: is an item present or the system functioning?

DECISION TREES

Back in the early days of personal computers, when graphical displays began to outnumber character-mode displays (and state-of-the-art computers had less processing power than modern smart phones yet took up most of your desk), a remarkable game came out that made those underpowered machines look like far more expensive graphical workstations.

The game was called **Doom** and it achieved its magic through a special incantation called binary space partitioning (BSP) trees. In essence, BSP trees enabled the game engine to quickly determine what the player was looking at so that it could ignore most of the information about the environment and focus the computer's meager processing power on rendering just those things the player could see.

Decision trees are an organizational tool that has much of the same magic as BSP trees. While there are more rigorous applications of decision trees, the basic idea is that you lay out a tree of possible outcomes for each decision. As you work through the tree, you can eliminate branches that lead to undesirable outcomes and the best course of action becomes clearer.

MOTIVATIONAL GAMES

When asked about their processes, many writers mention motivational games. The games generally follow the pattern of allowing the writer a reward if they produce some number of words, or write for a given amount of time, or send a number of submissions, and so on.

The best motivational games are little systems that help you move forward. The worst get in the way of what you're trying to accomplish.

Sometimes good games become a problem when you lose perspective. There are two insidious ways to lose perspective:

1. the game interferes with doing real work
2. the game becomes something that adds to your burden of guilt and makes you too depressed to do real work

So, how do you keep your motivational games in perspective?

This is a skill you'll have to develop on your own because we're all susceptible to different distractions and modes of procrastination: one size of advice doesn't fit all. But here's an example to get you started.

While drafting a novel, I often play a game to build momentum. My goal is daily progress, not a particular number of words. So I count the day as a successful writing day if I write at least a hundred new words. The game is to see how many consecutive days I can count as writing days. It may not sound like much, but this game helps me focus on steady progress during periods when my available writing time is constrained.

WRITE IT DOWN

It's important to have a simple and consistent way to capture ideas as they arise and hold them until you have time to act upon them.

Why?

Psychologists say the average person can only keep track of seven things at a time. If something new requires your attention, then one of the seven things you're currently tracking falls off the list—which is why it's probably no accident seven is a holy number in many cultures.

I always try to keep pen and paper nearby. Some people like notebooks or bound journals because they want a record of their ideas. I prefer my Clipboard of Power—a sleek, all-aluminum device that never runs down its batteries and is almost as stylish as the fruit-themed products from a certain computer company in California—and a stack of scratch paper.

Where the relative permanence of binding in notebooks calls for something significant, scratch paper is expendable and so it doesn't matter what or how I write. But an obligation (or lack thereof) to write something significant is only half the story: I use my scratch paper as a temporary repository to hold the idea only long enough for me to act upon it.

* * *

The point of little systems is not to take away your responsibility to think but to help you simplify complex situations. Finding ways to simplify what you need to do in time and space is actually a creative challenge. After all, the most effective art has an elegant simplicity. Why not strive for the same level of artistic elegance as you manage your affairs?

CHAPTER 29.

THE ART OF DOING HARD THINGS

There's an old mining lament about loading sixteen tons—"and whadda ya get? Another day older, and deeper in debt."

One ton is 2,000 pounds, so sixteen tons is 32,000 pounds.

That sounds overwhelming.

Over the course of an eight-hour workday, however, you'd only need to load 4,000 pounds (two tons) an hour to reach a sixteen-ton quota.

That still sounds like a lot.

If you could load 100 pounds in a minute—say, thirty-three pounds every twenty seconds—it would only take forty minutes to load 4,000 pounds and you'd have time for a twenty minute break every hour.

There's no question it would take strength and stamina to keep loading all day. But after we break it down, the overwhelming job is actually manageable.

Writing a novel is a lot like loading sixteen tons: in general, you've got to produce somewhere between 60,000 and 100,000 words. That sounds like a lot. But if you break it down to 1,000 words a day (and keep up the pace) you'll finish a draft of your novel in two or three months.

Like the journey of a thousand miles that begins with a single step, you'll be surprised at what you can accomplish if you consistently move your project forward by a doable, sustainable amount each day.

SMALL STEPS AND MILESTONES

When I graduated from college, I was paralyzed by the thought of picking a career. I simply couldn't imagine doing anything for forty years. The scope was overwhelming.

But I could imagine doing something for four years. After all, I'd just completed an undergraduate degree. So I stopped trying to find a career-scale answer and instead attacked the problem in four year chunks.

It wasn't the first time I learned the lesson of taking down overwhelming problems by breaking them into manageable chunks. There's real power in saying, "I don't know if I can do all of it, but I can do this part." Repeat the heads-down process of dealing with manageable chunks often enough and you'll be amazed at how much the formerly overwhelming problem has shrunk when you come up for air.

And when you come up for air, take a moment to acknowledge milestones.

Graduations, anniversaries, the odometer rolling over—these are all opportunities to pause and recognize our progress. Some people find this difficult, so let me hasten to add that it's important to take stock of what you've actually done, not what you hoped to do.

If I'm careful, and realistic, I'm often pleasantly

surprised by how much I've done. Of course, it's never as much as I hoped I'd do, but it's always better than I feared.

Don't underestimate the power of small steps. If you chip away a little each day, in time you'll look up and realize that you've moved a mountain.

EAT YOUR VEGETABLES FIRST

My son has a curious but not uncommon habit: he eats his food in order, starting with what he likes best. This means he often ends with a lonely pile of something green—peas or lettuce—on his plate and a court order not to leave the table until it's gone.

I wasn't terribly fond of vegetables when I was his age. At some point, though, I discovered my problem wasn't the vegetables—or the non-sweet fruits like tomatoes, cucumber, squash, peppers, etc. that people often lump in with vegetables—but the taste that lingered in my mouth after I ate them. Once I began taking care to finish up with something neutral to clear my palette, I found I actually enjoyed vegetables.

Motivational games tied to milestones are one way to make an unpleasant task palatable. Another is to break the task into smaller, more pleasant sub-tasks. But the real trick is to find the root cause—what is it that makes the task unpleasant—and then come up with a way of addressing the root cause, like my discovery about eating vegetables.

DOING WHAT NEEDS TO BE DONE

Sometimes the only way to get something done is to, "cowboy up," or, "pull up your big boy pants," and do it.

Perhaps that sounds a bit glib, but it's surprising how

often people try to deal with their problems by hoping they'll go away or wishing that someone else would solve them. They do everything in their power to avoid doing what's in their power to do about the problem.

It's a difficult technique to master because of the constant, overwhelming temptation to give up.

Of course, I'm not arguing for pigheadedness or ignorantly plowing ahead. I'm simply saying that sometimes the best solution to a problem is to stop worrying, roll up your sleeves, and get to work.

HOW TO TAKE RESPONSIBILITY

Taking responsibility doesn't mean accepting blame. Blame is about shifting responsibility. Taking responsibility means getting past blame and asking hard questions like, "What did I learn from that situation and what will I do differently next time?"

Unfortunately, learning to take responsibility is particularly difficult in our society because we're taught, early and often, that it's much easier to avoid responsibility. For example, every time there's a problem, someone says, "There ought to be a law." The more laws we add, the more responsibility we shift to the government and the regulators.

The tendency to claim that we are exceptions is even more insidious. A great many people think they should be excused because they belong to a disadvantaged group. Please understand: I know that life isn't fair, that people do a great job of being crappy to each other, and there are a great many wrongs that should be righted. But you're going to have to wait a long time for things to get better if you don't ever ask yourself, "Is there anything I can do?"

The best problem solvers are more concerned with

how to go forward than with who caused the problem. The history of the failure is only important to the degree that it shows the way to the solution. In other words, they take positive responsibility to resolve the matter.

* * *

Much of what we celebrate as creativity is really the result of someone who was willing to take creative responsibility, do the hard work that needed to be done, and make it all look effortless. While focusing on the moment of inspiration makes for a better story, Thomas Edison—a creative fellow in his own right—captured the true essence of creativity when he gave us the ninety-nine to one percent ratio between perspiration and inspiration.

CHAPTER 30.

MAKING TIME

How do you find time to write?

Actually, time finds you, whether you're ready or not. You can never find time, you can only make it.

So how do you make time to write?

At one level, it simply comes down to the question, "What are you willing to give up in order to write?" Of course, saying it that way makes you sound less than committed if you're not a writing hermit.

So how can a person who has a life outside of writing make time?

PRIORITIES

Many of us treat our writing as a hobby—not that we're lacking in commitment but rather that we approach it more like a leisure activity. Let me hasten to add that there's nothing wrong with writing as a hobby if you're satisfied with the time you are able to devote to it. If, however, you wish you had more time to write, raising the priority of your writing to the same level as, say, eating, means it's no longer optional.

Sandra Tayler said, "When I write first, the laundry gets easier."

TIME SAVERS

Now that you've raised its priority, you can make time for your writing by spending less of it on other things. There's an entire industry devoted to offering products, services, and advice to save time. I've found ways to save a surprising amount of time by creating little systems to streamline recurring tasks. For example, I sort mail (the paper kind) over the garbage can because most of it will end up there.

I have other little systems for mail that help me apply the principle of handling things once. Any mail that I can't throw away or deal with immediately goes into a file that holds it until the day I need to act on it. With this system, I never need to spend time or waste mental energy on things that can't be taken care of for a few days.

The most effective sort of streamlining is to remove decision points. If you like to write in the morning, but find it hard because of the time it takes you to get ready for the day, choosing your clothes the night before means one less decision to make in the morning.

I mention these systems as examples of ways to make more time available for writing. You will, of course, have to figure out what works for you. The beauty of little systems is that they take so little effort to set up that you can try something for awhile. If it doesn't work or needs to be changed, you can do so because you don't have a significant investment in the system.

CLEAR BOTH PHYSICAL AND TEMPORAL SPACE

Creativity is a safe, adult-appropriate word for play. In order to sustain the focus needed to create long-form works, you need both time and space to play. You need a place where you can leave your half-built castles in the air while attending to other things secure in the knowledge that they'll still be there, undisturbed and ready to play with, when you return.

In this age of convenient mobile computing systems, setting up your writing environment may be no more complicated than opening a laptop and firing up a word processor. Clearing your schedule and your internal worry processor are more difficult. This is why many people like to write in a neutral place like a library or a cafe. Whatever you do, the key is to find a time and space where you can focus on your project.

CREATE STABILITY

Emergencies will derail your writing. You can't prevent all emergencies, but you can take care of things under your control so that you're not creating problems for yourself.

If, for example, you paid your bills when you received your statement, you'd never run the risk of leaving it all to the last moment and then having a fire drill to get everything paid. I know people who, as a matter of principle, pay their bills at the last possible moment in order to deny the billing entity whatever interest it might have earned from having the money a few days earlier. I prefer to discharge my obligations as soon as they come due so that I can devote the time I would have spent keeping track of my unpaid bills to my writing, secure in the knowledge that it's safe to play.

WRITING IS A HABIT

In a discussion about managing weight I overheard someone who said:

Eating one piece of cake doesn't make you fat.
Not eating one piece of cake doesn't make you thin.

The same is true of writing:

Writing one day doesn't make you a writer.
Not writing one day doesn't mean you cease to be a writer.

Writing, in case you haven't noticed, is habit forming. As with other habits, there are good ones and bad ones. Bad writing habits are the ones that may give you a rush for a while, but overall tend to leave you feeling guilty and depressed. Good writing habits may have less of a rush but produce a general feeling of satisfaction.

Does this sound uncomfortably like food habits?

It's no accident because the psychology is similar. Studies show that we systematically choose short term benefits over our long term objectives because we believe we can and will do better tomorrow.

Another point that came up in the conversation about managing weight was that you can't change a lifetime of accumulated habits overnight, but you can change one thing today.

If you aspire to write but can't seem to make the time, you're not going to change all the habits that make it hard to make time overnight. What you can do, however, is to choose to write instead of doing something else when you have a few minutes.

Think of it as the writing equivalent of not having a second piece of cake. If that becomes a habit, then in time you may no longer need the first piece of cake (i.e, you may find it easier to make a bit more time to write). If you can stop dreaming about your bestseller (and getting depressed because your draft isn't even close), and think instead in terms of small steps and milestones, you'll be amazed at the effect even a small change can have over time.

After all, writing is a habit.

CHAPTER 31.

REPEATABILITY

The final, and most important, phase of the scientific method is to repeat the experiment at different times and in different places in order to show that it produces the same results. Art is not science and a creative endeavor may be as ephemeral as a sand castle against the tide, but repeatability is what distinguishes true creativity from a happy accident.

This is not to say that you must become a creative automaton. Rather, it's about overcoming the fear that having succeeded once you won't be able to do it again.

ON THE SECOND BOOK FUNK

Authors often have a major crisis of confidence when they start their second book. They're haunted by the fear that they had only the one book in them and will never again be able to produce anything as good.

Why are writers susceptible to such fears?

Putting on my amateur therapist goatee and breaking out the bubble pipe, we have not one but two potential pitfalls awaiting us when we finish a project. The first is psychological and the second structural. They're a nasty pair because they feed off of each other. And if you're not careful, you'll find yourself immobilized.

THE PSYCHOLOGICAL PROBLEM

It's easy to believe you've become something different than you were when you started your first project. In other professions, one can use a title only after a significant and demonstrable achievement. Lawyers have bar exams. Doctors have medical school, internships, and residencies. Many other professions also can't be practiced without a license. It's natural to assume that a published book is the writer's equivalent of professional certification.

After completing the arduous process of turning ideas into prose, polishing the manuscript, and persevering through the publishing process, you have every right to think you've accomplished something significant. When you've done that, it's natural to believe you've learned something and are better at what you do.

The net effect is a tendency to believe that now you're good.

You may have given yourself license to suck when you were starting out, but with a published book you're beyond that, right?

So you bang out the first few pages of the new project and ... they're not very good. And suddenly you have to question everything you assumed about your new identity.

THE STRUCTURAL PROBLEM

The more fundamental mistake is forgetting the process

by which you created your first book: the multiple drafts, the rounds of revisions, and the hours spent agonizing over a word or phrase.

You'll only succeed in depressing yourself if you compare your new project to the book you just finished. A project that's only a month old will always look primitive compared to one you've revised and polished for a year or two.

If you must compare something, compare first drafts. Chances are you'll find that the first draft for your second project is a bit better than the first draft for your first project.

SO WHAT CAN YOU DO?

Doctors, who have real credentials, practice medicine. Writers would do well to follow that example: we should see ourselves not as someone who possesses some expertise but as someone who practices the art of refining words into stories through a patient process.

PLAYING

The concept of practice is all well and good, but how do you practice creativity?

You play.

Play, not to be confused with recreation, is the primary way in which children learn about their world. From babbling babies, who are, in fact, experimenting with vocalizations, to children dressing up and inventing imaginary worlds in which they can try on adult roles, play is about figuring out what and how things work.

Growed-ups are distinguished from the livelier, younger lot, in part because of the degree to which they have forgotten how to play. We forget how to play on purpose as we become adults because play is more often about failure than success. A large part of being an adult is about control, so most of us believe we can't afford to fail: we may say that too many people depend on us, but the deeper problem is that failure undermines our sense of who we are because it means we're not in control.

Creativity and the creative life are fundamentally about play, which means they involve a great deal more trying and failing than most other adult endeavors. The single greatest key to having more creativity in your life is to cultivate a fundamental playfulness that enables you to set aside your self-consciousness about failure.

And when you stop worrying about failing, creative repeatability will come naturally.

CHAPTER 32.

A CREATIVE LIFE IS THE SUM OF ALL YOUR PARTS

With many things in life, the best way to learn something is to jump in and try to do it. This is particularly true for writing. Slamming words together on a regular basis—and in a way that makes sense to someone else—is harder than it looks: it's certainly much harder than reading tamed words lined up smartly in a row and showing no sign of the struggle required to beat them into submission. The best way to truly appreciate the nature of the work involved is to try and do it.

Once you've tried putting words together to express your ideas, you can learn a lot by reading the work of other authors and seeing how they handled similar problems. You'll also learn a lot about conventions, clichés, and reader expectations. But don't confine your reading to your genre. Read widely—it's the best way to keep your idea pump primed.

Having repeated the orthodox answer, it's time to confess that for all my reading and writing, I really learned to write by watching TV, composing music, and developing software.

READING AND WRITING

I read and wrote a lot when I was young. Indeed, I did so much reading and writing that they became a constant part of my life as I did other things. I got very good at academic and technical writing. But my attempts at fiction were less than satisfactory.

SOFTWARE

Meanwhile, I was developing software. There are thousands (sometimes millions) of things that have to be right in order to get a non-trivial piece of software working. It's overwhelming unless you can see the larger patterns and relationships. Working with software taught me about balancing abstraction and concrete implementation, and how to move across concerns at multiple levels of magnitude without getting lost.

A writer must be able to do the same thing, keeping in mind where the current section and chapter and part and book are all going while crafting the current paragraph to do its job in a way that supports all the other levels.

MUSIC

There's a strong connection between writing and music because both forms of expression are experienced linearly. I've composed a fair amount of music for my own use. Doing so has given me some feel for theme, motif, tension, resolution, anticipation, and direction. Music has the added benefit that you can figure out whether a song is going somewhere interesting more quickly than you can with a novel.

TELEVISION

So how did I learn to write from television (a medium that hardly seems to belong in the same sentence with the phrase, "great literature,")?

I watched **Babylon 5**.

And as I watched, I also followed along on the Internet as J. Michael Straczynski, executive producer and primary writer for **Babylon 5,** described what he was doing over the roughly seven years from the pilot to the final episode. I found it immensely enlightening to read what Straczynski said he was trying to do in an episode and then to see how it actually played out. I was finally able to see concrete examples of things like character development and multiple themes woven into a larger story arc.

* * *

Of course, when we're talking about, "writing," we're talking more about storytelling than how you put words together. When it's time for the final tally, how you learned to tell a story will matter much less than whether you can tell a good one. The techniques that enable you to use your chosen medium skillfully are simply ways to reduce the distance between creative conception and expression. And the most important element of creativity is the unique essence you bring to the equation.

PART IV.

ARTISAN PUBLISHING

CHAPTER 33.

ARTISAN PUBLISHING

"May you live in interesting times," is an old Chinese curse, and sounds tame, as curses go, compared to ones that call down withering diseases, plagues of vermin, and the wrath of the undead. Its beauty, however, is that it looks innocuous, but packs a wallop: unlike the gruesome specificity of the typical curses *interesting times* could mean anything.

Regardless of the cause, times become interesting when old certainties no longer hold and no one knows what to do. Publishing is now in the midst of interesting times. For a substantial portion of the last century and most of the first decade of this one, the publishing industry has been defined by the logistics of distributing books to bookstores. There were innovations, like mass-market paperbacks and book stands in supermarkets and big-box retailers, but none of these changed the fundamental distribution pattern. Setting yourself up as a publisher required a second-mortgage-level investment to print books and a tremendous amount of legwork to arrange for distribution. The advent of electronic publishing changed everything because the barrier to entry dropped to little more than the time and effort required to write the book.

What we used to call publishing (or commercial publishing if we needed to distinguish the standard model, where authors were paid by publishers, from vanity publishing, where authors paid publishers) now gets qualified with words like, traditional, legacy, or even, dinosaur. And now we talk about self-publishing and independent or *indie* publishing (an attempt to align with the success and credibility of independently produced films and music), and even argue that trading a 70% royalty for a 15% royalty and recognition by a publisher is a new kind of vanity publishing.

But there's something happening in the market that is far more important than the tug-of-war between dependent and independent publishing models.

THE LITERARY MARKET OPENS UP

Responding to a question in an interview on the **Guide to Literary Agents** blog about what had changed in the publishing industry during the last decade, agent Jessica Regel said:

> "I'm sure writers have been hearing this for years, I know I have, but the quiet, steady mid-list book is dying. It's extremely difficult to sell a quiet, well-written book. Each project I go out with needs to have that one-line movie pitch. It's all about the hook—paired with phenomenal writing." [1]

It's easy to hear that, "It's extremely difficult to sell a quiet, well-written book," shake our heads knowingly, and grumble about publishing following in the footsteps other entertainment industries that focus on blockbusters. Regel's comment, however, is evidence of a fundamental structural change rumbling, like shifting tectonic plates, through the industry.

In 1997, Clayton Christensen published, **The Innovator's Dilemma: When New Technologies Cause Great Firms to Fail**, [2] in which he explored the generational pattern where once dominant firms are eventually eclipsed by more nimble startups that, in turn, become dominant. According to common wisdom, the old firms became dinosaurs for whom the meteor couldn't come too soon because their management failed to keep up with changing technology. Christensen's research uncovered something far stranger: the firms that failed were generally well managed—listening to their customers, investing in research and development, and aggressively marketing their innovations—and yet none of that staved off their eventual demise.

The problem, though, is structural. Christensen showed how, across many industries, companies consistently migrate to the high end of the market where their products enjoy the greatest profit margin. In doing so, they often abandon the low end to new firms with new technology. The key piece in the puzzle that Christensen brought to light was the fact that established firms could rationally abandon the low end of the market because the new technology was so obviously inferior to the older technology the established firms controlled. For example, the manufacturers of 5.25 inch hard drives had nothing to worry about when 3.5 inch hard drives were introduced because the smaller disks were slower and held less data: they were only good for laptops, where space was at a premium. But things tend to get better over time, and in a few years the smaller hard drives were good enough that computer manufacturers standardized on them for both laptop and desktop systems, and suddenly the market for 5.25 inch hard drives evaporated.

What does this have to do with publishing?

The disappearance of mid-list books from agents' radar is clear evidence of publishers moving toward the high end of the book market and abandoning the low end: it's no longer worth the time or effort to bring a quiet, mid-list book to market when what publishers really need is a string of bestsellers.

E-books and online markets provide an inferior, but cheaper reading experience. It's a textbook example of disruptive innovation.

Of course, printed books and the established firms that produce them are not going to go away—at least not anytime soon. Books will continue to be available in a vibrant mix of print and electronic formats. But it's not hard to imagine a time when printed books, like vinyl records, are only sought out by true aficionados.

The way in which the forces at work in the market for books will ultimately play out is much less important than the fact that established firms are moving toward the high-end of the market, creating space at the low end for smaller, newer firms and even for artisans.

That would be enough to qualify as interesting times, but there is another, equally fundamental, structural shift at work in the market.

THE END OF ARTIFICIAL SCARCITY

I stopped going to first-run movies a long time ago. I made that decision during the era of local video-rental stores. The fact that I would eventually be able to see the movie, at a cost that was easier to bear on my starving-student budget, took the wind of urgency out of my movie-watching sails.

Now, the same thing has happened with books.

There's more to the analogy between book-buying and movie-going: both industries do their best business with blockbuster releases because they create value by creating artificial scarcity. Being among the first to see a much anticipated movie or read a major author's latest release gives short term benefits, above and beyond the value of the story, like bragging rights.

The Internet is well on its way to making anything instantly available. One of the consequences of instant availability is that being first in line to get something the moment it's released becomes less important. Elizabeth Gumport said:

> "Newness is not a fixed property. There must be a less arbitrary, more sensible way to encounter books ... one which doesn't foreground mediocrities simply because they are the newest mediocrities. 'Recent' is not a synonym for 'relevant.'" [3]

Libraries, the antithesis of theaters and bookstores, are fundamentally about lasting value—not in terms of absolute worth but in the much simpler sense of something in which people continue to find value over time. The challenge for authors and publishers in the brave new electronic world will be to create lasting value that attracts an ever growing audience instead of relying on scarcity to create a bubble of demand around the release.

WHAT IS ARTISAN PUBLISHING?

The opening of the literary market and the end of artificial scarcity has created an opportunity for a new kind of publisher: an artisan publisher.

The word, artisan, long carried the sense of the common practitioner, as opposed to the artist who brought genius and inspiration to the work. But as mass production blesses us with a collective and mostly uniform affluence, artisan has come to signify a means of production where low unit cost and economies of scale are not the primary objective. Artisan bread, for example, is made by hand even though there are bread factories that can out-produce an army of bakers.

Why, if we are rational economic actors, would we ever choose a product that is more expensive and less available than a mass-produced equivalent? People who prefer artisan breads may argue in terms of the varieties or flavors available nowhere else, or the virtue of supporting local production, but for most people it simply tastes better. Small production batches and traditional, hand-made methods allow skilled craftspeople to invest love, care, and attention to detail to insure the integrity of their work.

Artisan publishing isn't simply a variation on the theme of doing it yourself. The large, well-stocked home improvement centers dotting our suburban landscape owe their existence more to naivety, false economy, and hubris than to a genuine and supportable conviction that doing it yourself is the best way to get the job done well, right, and in a timely fashion. The path of an artisan publisher begins with having something worth saying and a thorough effort to determine the best way to publish that work. As with our writing, where no character, scene, or sentence is too precious to escape scrutiny, artisan publishing has nothing to do with shortcuts or showing the gatekeepers how wrong they were about your manuscript and everything to do with what is best and right for the project.

WHAT DO YOU CARE ABOUT?

One of the most important lessons every skilled craftsperson must learn is just because you can doesn't mean you should. The greatest works of art are exercises in restraint not excess.

Artisan publishing is a patient, laborious path. It's not enough to have the skill, the aptitude, or even the inclination to publish your own material. You need to know why, both for your particular project and for you as an individual, the way of the artisan is worth all the time and trouble it will cost you.

A journey of a thousand miles may well begin with a single step, but your chances of completing the roughly two million steps that comprise the journey are poor if you don't know why you're doing it. There are many bad reasons—one of the worst being because everyone else is doing it—and only a few good ones. The difference is that bad reasons wear away over time but good ones will see you through to the end.

No true craftsperson undertakes a work lightly—not because their work has mystical significance but because the hallmark of skill is to act deliberately. In order to act deliberately you need to know why you're acting: you need to have a sense of your mission as an artisan publisher. Otherwise, you'll provide yet another confirmation of the old aphorism that if you're aiming at nothing you'll hit it.

WHY THIS GUIDE?

There are already too many books promising to give you the insider secrets that will enable you to make a fortune in electronic publishing—how to format and upload text, create covers, and build a readership with free, or cheap books, and paid reviews that will make your e-books fly off the virtual shelves.

This guide covers none of that: it's not a how-to, it's a why-to. It's a guide to the context, philosophy, and expectations you should have if you want to be an artisan publisher. Chapter two sets the groundwork with a clear view of the publishing industry because you need to understand what commercial publishers actually do and the roles of author and publisher if you want to participate intelligently. Chapter three takes a sober look at the reasons you shouldn't choose artisan publishing. Having laid that groundwork, chapter four explores the advantages of being an artisan publisher, the biggest of which, editorial control, is covered in chapter five. Chapter six turns to the challenges you'll likely face as an artisan publisher. Managing time and your expectations about time is enough of a challenge, in its own right, that it is the subject of chapter seven. Chapter eight outlines aspects of the craft of publishing you will need to master. The artisan philosophy of business and marketing are covered in chapters nine and ten, respectively. Chapter eleven dismantles the illusion of a national book culture that holds back many potential artisans. Chapter twelve explores strategic publishing in an age of abundance (what some have called the problem of discoverability). And chapter thirteen steps back to put the entire discussion into perspective.

* * *

The electronic frontier is neither literary heaven nor hell. It's simply a new set of opportunities for readers and writers. It's not a religion that requires you to renounce other forms of publishing. Rational authors, acting in their best business interests and in light of their particular circumstances, will find good reasons to take advantage of all the different publishing options at various times and places.

The barriers to entry are low enough that you will likely find reasons to participate, but don't confuse the ease with which you can publish with lower standards. In this new age of digital abundance, the one thing that matters—which is the only thing that has ever mattered—is writing a good book.

CHAPTER 34.

A CLEAR VIEW OF THE PUBLISHING INDUSTRY

It has become fashionable, among people who publish independently, to characterize the preceding generation of publishers, particularly the large commercial houses centered in New York City, as dinosaurs. And for those of us coming to the game from the perspective of readers or writers there is much about a business devoted to moving large stacks of paper between warehouses and bookstores that seems counterintuitive.

The aura of rebelliousness is an undeniable part of the allure of independent publishing. Freed from the shackles of the old monolithic system, nothing stands between us and the successful realization of our dreams. The rules of the old guard were made to be broken.

Except the ones that weren't.

One of the sad lessons revolutionaries get to learn is that much of the structure of the system they overthrew was in place not because of the tyranny, veniality, or shortsightedness of the former overlords but because it was a necessary part of government. Similarly, there are things about publishing that are there not because of the whims of elitist cultural gatekeepers but for reasons ranging from economics to readers expectations.

There are structural reasons for some of the patterns of publishing that you should understand if you're going to venture into the same space.

THE GEOLOGY OF PUBLISHING

Just as many of us suffer from innumeracy—the inability to think rationally about large numbers—many of us also suffer from ahistoricity, the tendency to assume that if something has been a certain way for a long time that's how it's supposed to be.

There were all sorts of publishing options in the nineteenth century: Mark Twain, for example, pre-sold his books by subscription through door-to-door salesman [4] and Charles Dickens serialized his novels in affordable monthly booklets [5].

The current system of large publishers with well integrated supply chains feeding a legion of booksellers is a relatively recent development in the grand history of publishing. The U.S. model was established during the Great Depression in the 1930s, when publishers allowed bookstores to essentially sell on consignment by returning unsold titles instead of purchasing non-returnable books for resale. The need to finance the returns system favored larger publishers with deeper pockets over smaller ones. And the shift from outright sales to sell–through intensified the need to produce certain kinds of *commercial* books at the expense of other kinds of books. The overall drift of the publishing industry is analogous to the rise of vast industrial farms full of specialized machinery optimized for single crop.

TRADITIONAL PUBLISHERS ARE REALLY TRADE PUBLISHERS

Whether we call the new mode of publishing self, indie, or artisan, the label used most commonly for the formerly dominant publishing model is *traditional*. As people who work with words, we understand how important it is to use the right ones. There are, for example, some circles in which the word traditional means, "time-tested values," not, "hopelessly stuck in the past." But the real problem with calling commercial publishing *traditional* isn't whether it implies the business model is good or bad but that it doesn't accurately describe the business model.

Major commercial publishers are actually trade publishers. They publish to the book trade, which means they sell their wares to booksellers, not readers.

"Wait," you may object, "readers are still the ones buying the books, so what's the big deal?"

The fundamental problem of selling children's books is that children don't buy them. Practically all children's books are purchased by well-meaning adults. A children's book must, therefore, appeal both to the child for whom it's intended and also to someone in the circle of adults who have an interest in supplying that child with reading material. The two constituencies, children and adults, often have very different reasons for choosing a book.

Booksellers, of course, want to sell books. The ideal book for a bookseller is one that every reader wants and will line up to buy. Readers want to buy books that will entertain, educate, or give them an experience they value. The ideal book for a reader is one that speaks to his or her specific needs and desires. Absent that ideal book, readers choose books from the bookseller's selection that seem most likely to meet their needs. The two constituencies (booksellers and readers) often have very different reasons for choosing a book.

What all of this means is that publishers are in the business of convincing booksellers to stock their books. They don't deal directly with readers. Convincing readers to buy their books is, at best, a secondary concern for trade publishers.

PUBLISHERS ARE RISK AGGREGATORS

Coming to publishing from a career in high-tech, I couldn't help noticing the similarities between publishers and venture capitalists. Both, for example, take the lion's share of the equity and leave you with ten to fifteen percent of the business.

The similarity isn't accidental. Like venture capital, most media businesses—books, movies, music—are structured as risk aggregators.

"No," you say, "publishing is about culturally relevant ideas, experiences, and expressions. It's full of people who love books, not actuaries."

Perhaps, but staffing is a by-product of the economic logic of the business model.

Look at it this way: if you were presented with an opportunity to gamble on something that offered a massive payoff but required a substantial bet and had payoff odds of one in a hundred (i.e., you're going to lose your money ninety-nine times out of a hundred), and you could only afford to make the bet once, would you risk the money?

But if you and ninety-nine of your closest friends pooled your resources—and if the payoff was greater than the hundred bets you'd have to make—instead of squandering your money, the proposition becomes a sure thing.

Venture capitalists invest expecting seven out of the ten companies to fail, two to break even, and only one to succeed—where success means returning enough to cover the other bets and provide a profit. Publishers work in a similar fashion: most books don't earn out their advances, some (the mid-listers) provide a modest return, and a few produce stratospheric profits that cover the losses on all the other books as well as temporarily satisfying the shareholders' appetites.

As an author, part of what you're giving up when you sign a contract with a publisher that gives you an advance is the risk that even though you're good enough to get published your book might not sell well enough to provide a return on your effort. During the heyday of the advance system, which subsidized writers by decoupling compensation and sales, publishers aggregated the risk individual authors took in writing their books—not because they were charitable but because developing talent reduced the publisher's risk over time.

So why are publishing companies structured as risk aggregators?

Because no one—absolutely no one—knows what books will sell.

WRITERS ARE FUNGIBLE

All of this exposes a deep structural irony: writers, the life-blood of the publishing industry—the only people in the business with whom readers make an emotional connection—are, insofar as publishers are concerned, interchangeable resources. In economic term, they are fungible.

Kristine Kathryn Rusch explains it this way:

"Contrary to what you've always believed, traditional publishing companies have never cared about writers. Traditional publishers know that when one writer goes away, another will step into her place. You're a rotating group of widgets that might make the publisher some money. If you don't make the publisher money, then they'll find someone who will." [6]

As much as it sounds like simple, cynical exploitation, the writer's place at the bottom of the food chain is an inevitable consequence of publishers operating as risk aggregators. Each book they publish is a bet, and they know most bets won't pay off. They have no incentive to form a special relationship with an author until there's evidence that bet will pay off. As soon as there's evidence the bet is not going to pay off, publishers generally cut their losses and find someone else to bet on.

Insofar as the industry is concerned, writers are to publishers as ore is to miners: some books are gold and most are dross but no one knows which is which until the publisher refines them and puts them on the market.

Of course, the problem with the last sentence is the notion that publishers are necessary to turn the raw material of a manuscript into something more marketable. It was closer to the truth in the last century, when publishers controlled the physical process of printing and distributing books. Now publishers have outsourced much of the editorial development (to agents and freelancers, further reducing the opportunities to develop a relationship with your publisher) and all of the printing and distribution operations. What's left is a risk aggregation company in which you, the author, are a number, not a name, until your bet pays off.

This is not as grim as it sounds. If you can produce commercially successful books, publishers are your best friends because they can distribute your book everywhere and they will happily laugh all the way to the bank with you.

If you can't produce the kind of books they want, the good news is that there are now other options.

But why would any writer enter into such a lopsided relationship?

THE SEPARATE ROLES OF AUTHORS AND PUBLISHERS

The broad-brush functional differences between the right and left hemispheres of the brain have become a mainstay of pop psychology: the right brain is the seat of creativity while the left brain handles detail work. Some people personify the two as the artist and the accountant in your head. While that simple dichotomy isn't supported by our growing understanding of neuroscience, it is a useful way to characterize the traditional division of labor between author and publisher. It's easy to see the author as artist in contrast to—and sometimes in conflict with—the publisher as accountant and business manager.

As with most common notions, this analogy has a kernel of truth: authors provide the novel (in both senses of the word) content and publishers take care of the details involved in preparing, packaging, and presenting that content in the marketplace.

Of course, the divide isn't between creative and non-creative work. Writing involves plenty of drudgery and business often requires creativity. But there is an important distinction between the kinds of creative and detail work that are most effective in the traditional roles of author and publisher.

Writing is a conceptual act of centralization: all of your efforts focus on pulling discrete ideas together and arranging them to create a coherent whole. Promotion is conceptually decentralized: you push the book out through as many distinct channels and tailor the message to fit as many different constituencies as possible.

Unfortunately, this right–brain/left–brain separation between authors and publishers has, even in the golden age of traditional publishing, been the exception, not the rule. Publishers generally expect most of their authors to shoulder the lion's share of the marketing effort beyond the book trade. After all the work of perfecting the manuscript, new authors are often surprised to learn they have to master an entirely different set of skills when the time comes to promote their book.

As challenging as it may be for an author with a traditional publishing arrangement to switch writing and marketing hats, self-publishing means you have to wear both hats all the time. If you choose to be an artisan publisher, you're actually signing up to bridge the traditional right-brain/left-brain split between authors and publishers in your own head.

If you dread the endless rounds of verifying fiddly grammar details that are an inescapable part of editing your book, wait until you're stuck trying to figure out why the formatting for your e-book is off on three devices but looks great everywhere else. In addition to the art, getting covers right requires attention to graphic file formats, image scale and resolution for different platforms, and a host of conventions like including your ISBN as a barcode on the back cover along with the book's category. Then there are details like copyright statements, warranties, and metadata that must accompany your book, all of which have to be both correct and correctly presented. Making sure all of these things are right requires constant checking and double checking.

Setting aside whatever frustration with the old or fascination with the new you may have, there are good reasons for the traditional division between producers and distributors in many sectors of the economy. You need to understand both the reasons for and the substance of each role if you want to walk the path of the artisan publisher because you're going to be doing both jobs.

CHAPTER 35.

WHY YOU SHOULDN'T CHOOSE ARTISAN PUBLISHING

Doing the right thing for the wrong reason is often as bad as doing the wrong thing. Many of the common reasons for becoming an artisan publisher are the wrong reasons. While the enviable success stories of writers who got nothing but rejections from agents and editors and then went on to become e-book millionaires suggest otherwise, artisan publishing is not a shortcut to fame, fortune, or vindication.

SHOW ME THE MONEY!

If you're toying with the notion of becoming an artisan publisher because you want to get rich quick, stop right now. There are many other ways to make money that take far less effort and produce a more timely return. Some people have indeed made their fortune writing books just like others have become wealthy by winning the lottery, but neither approach offers a predictable, repeatable path to instant riches.

In a world where entire factories are optimized to

produce as much of one thing as quickly as possible, the artisan's handcrafted approach can never compete purely on price. Of course, artisans can make a living but they will never enjoy the per-unit profits that can be generated by the economies of scale in a large operation.

You might argue that the old economy-of-scale distinction between artisans and major enterprises doesn't apply to electronic books because production costs have dropped to almost nothing: an artisan publisher can produce a high-quality book just as easily as a major publisher and, as a smaller operator with lower fixed costs, can afford to undercut the big houses on price.

But the changes that have opened up new prospects for artisan publishers have not erased the advantages held by large organizations. For example, established publishers continue to enjoy economies of scale in marketing and discoverability. And because they have a decades-long history of producing books for large audiences they have the attention of an army of reviewers and booksellers. You won't command the attention of as large an audience until you are equally well established.

Don't make the simplistic mistake, as you're dazzled by the prospect of a 70% royalty, of thinking all you have to do is sell 50,000 copies of a $2.99 book to earn a six-figure income. Even with a dedicated sales force and standing orders from bookstores, major publishers rarely sell 50,000 copies of a title. On average, books published nationally—which includes bestsellers—sell a few thousand copies.

You may sigh and ask, "Are you saying we should publish for love, not money?"

No. It's simply that the money will not come quickly.

But that's not a bad thing: unlike ancient artisans, who were paid once for their work and depended on the next commission for their continued livelihood, an artisan publisher gets paid every time someone buys another copy of the books in his or her catalog. In web terms, artisan publishing is all about the long tail—the slow growth in the value of an expanding collection of published work over time.

What this really means is that artisan publishing operates under a more traditional model than current publishers. Before most publishing houses became divisions in even larger media conglomerates they earned their sustaining income from their backlist—books published prior to the current year that were in print and on sale. Your goal as an artisan publisher is similar: to produce a steady stream of high quality content which will, in time, generate a steady stream of revenue.

There's money to be made as an artisan publisher, but it won't come quickly or all at once.

A PROPER COMEUPPANCE

When you began to believe your writing might actually be good enough to publish, you were determined to do everything right: you read writing books and blogs, went to conferences, found a critique group, polished your novel, researched agents, and sent the perfect query letter. And in return you heard nothing but silence— punctuated by the occasional rejection.

You did everything right and you weren't asking for special treatment, so why didn't you get some kind of response?

Even if you understand publishing is subjective, as time, rejections, and silence wear away your enthusiasm, it's hard not to suspect agents and editors of either conspiring to suppress your genius or being willfully ignorant.

Vengeance and vindication make a powerful motivational cocktail. Like many intoxicating substances, a little might help but a lot is a recipe for trouble: a desire for vindication may be good if it motivates you to finish and polish your project but leaping into artisan publishing because you're going to show all those shortsighted publishing professionals how wrong they were is a recipe for frustration and ultimately failure.

To begin with, the people who rejected or ignored you will probably never know that your project has been published because there are simply too many things being published for anyone to keep track of it all. Should they hear of your project they will likely give it little or no notice: agents and editors are looking for new material to sell.

The only thing guaranteed to get the attention of the gatekeepers is to release a book whose sales go off the charts. But even that won't convince an agent or editor she was wrong. Beyond subjectivity, there's so much serendipity in the process of producing and selling a book that having different people involved could produce wildly differing results: a different agent—your dream agent—might have sold the project to a different editor whose sensibilities might have colored the story just enough to miss striking a popular chord.

At a practical level, the slow, laborious path of artisan publishing means that you must invest a tremendous amount of work and patience into something where the odds of it making a splash in the market big enough to cause the gatekeepers even a twinge of regret are extremely small.

But the deeper truth is that artisan publishing is about love and devotion—which makes it fundamentally ill-suited for revenge.

SHORT-CIRCUITING THE GREAT CHAIN OF REJECTION

One of the down-sides of becoming an artisan publisher is that you must forego the luxury of getting rejected by agents and editors.

"A luxury?" you sputter.

Yes. Instead of the gentle buffeting you'll receive from publishing professionals, who respond with a polite, but vague, "It's not a good fit for us," you'll get slapped around by readers who have no qualms about telling the world they think your book is a piece of filth too vile even for a dung beetle.

As hard as it may be to believe, rejections from agents and editors offer several layers of comfort:

- They readily acknowledge their opinions are subjective and that perhaps someone else will like it.

- There's always the opportunity to revise: when you submit a manuscript to an agent or editor, you do so knowing they will generally ask for revisions.

- Agents and editors are always open to future submissions. If the piece you're shopping now isn't right for them your next one might be.

Compared to that, readers have no mercy:

- Most readers believe their opinions are objective, or at least representative: if they didn't like your book, why would anyone else.

- Readers expect a finished product. If they don't like your first version, they're not going to read your book a second time no matter how much you revise it.

- Readers hold grudges. If they hate one of your books, they'll likely hate the rest sight-unseen.

If you've turned to artisan publishing because you're tired of rejection you've come to the wrong place. Electronic publishing does let you bypass the gatekeepers who in the past might have kept you out of the market altogether. But the price for that access is that you also bypass the safety net those gatekeepers provide. If you're not careful, you open yourself up to getting rejected for everything from typos and grammar errors to characters and stories that don't resonate with readers.

Offering your work directly to readers requires more courage and a thicker skin than letting a publisher bring out your book. If you have a publisher and your book fails in the marketplace, you can always take consolation—whether it's true or not—in blaming them. When you publish your own work, you've got no one to blame but yourself.

If you can listen to readers rant that your loathsome book defiled the electrons used to store and transmit it and that you should be forcibly restrained from ever putting pen to paper, and then return to your writing with full confidence and vigor you've got what it takes to become an artisan publisher.

ON A MISSION FROM GOD

Jake and Elwood Blues, the titular characters in the movie **The Blues Brothers** (1980), left a trail of destruction in their wake as they tried to reunite their band for a benefit concert to save an orphanage. Their justification, which became one of the taglines for the movie, was, "We're on a mission from God."

The purer you believe your intentions to be, the more likely you are to leave a similar trail of carnage if you see artisan publishing as the way to fulfill your mission from God.

I know devout people who truly believe that God wants them to be rich so they can use their wealth to further God's purposes. Questions such as why God can't achieve his purposes directly or why, like the multitude of African princes soliciting strangers via email on the Internet, God needs to launder his money through their bank accounts never trouble them: amassing wealth is obviously what God wants them to do.

If you want to self-publish because you are God's messenger or because you know this is how God wants you to make the fortune that you will then dedicate to his greater glory, I have bad news for you: you're not alone. Many other people publishing their work have a similar conviction—and for the most part, it hasn't worked so well for them. You, of course, know that your case will be different because you are the only true messenger. Sadly, however, the vast majority of us won't be able to tell the difference between your true message and all the other false ones.

Those of you who are humble enough to leave God out of it, but needed to publish because you're smarter, can explain more clearly, or simply produce better work than anything else out there are actually in the same boat: the S.S. Hey-look-at-me. You've allowed the excellence of your work to blind you to the bedrock truth you must understand if you want to be an artisan publisher: it's not about you. Readers will only pick up your book if they believe it provides them value.

Keith Cronin said:

> "I remember whining to my mom many years ago about how hard my life was as a musician.... At some point in my monologue, Mom finally cut me off, with one simple sentence: "Keith," she said, "nobody ever asked you to do this."[7]

The daily mantra of a true artisan publisher is, "No one asked me to do this; I do this because I love it."

And if you still truly believe you're on a mission from God, please get a second opinion.

JACK OF ALL TRADES, MASTER OF NONE

For the vast majority of our history as a species, humans were content to live in relatively small groups and spend their time hunting and gathering—and no wonder: most hunter-gatherers work about twenty hours a week to get their living. Yet in the last 10,000-year blink of the evolutionary eye we suddenly have cities and civilizations exploding all over the planet. The culprit, according to anthropologists, is the specialization made possible by agricultural surpluses.

The power of specialization is obvious to every writer who dreams of walking away from the oppression of a day job and devoting his or her full-time to the craft. Imagine all the books you could write if you weren't limited to an hour or two of writing each day.

If you think artisan publishing offers a shortcut to becoming a full-time writer, I have bad news for you: artisan publishing is actually a shortcut to becoming a full-time publisher.

The difference between a writer who is published and a publisher who writes begins with the contrast between the passive phrase, "a writer who is published," and the active phrase, "a publisher who writes." One of the reasons for the traditional separation between authors and publishers is that it allows each partner to specialize.

There's so much to do as an artisan publisher that you can't afford to specialize. Serious writers understand how much time and effort it takes to go from an idea to a finished manuscript. Publishers understand how much time and effort it takes to go from a finish manuscript to a sellable book. You've got to be a generalist if you're going to do everything that needs to be done between the idea and the finished book. Even if you engage freelance editors and designers you still need to understand enough of what they do to be able to review and approve their work.

But it's worse than that. You actually need to become a serial specialist. Many of the nontrivial tasks—like writing and design—require focus and skill. And yet just as you're getting the hang of it you need to move on to something else. In practice this means you're constantly relearning things. If you feel like you're being pulled in too many different directions when you try to write now, you'll find artisan publishing more frustrating than fulfilling.

BE CAREFUL WHAT YOU WISH FOR

The problem with asking a child what they want to be when they grow up is that they can only see the cool parts of the job—they have no idea how much work it takes to become something or how much drudgery there is between the exciting bits. Firefighters, for example, spend more time sitting in the firehouse waiting for something to happen than racing through town, lights flashing and sirens wailing, in their special trucks.

As we grow, we learn that wishes often come with a price. In W. W. Jacobs' classic 1902 story, "The Monkey's Paw," a family receives the titular talisman along with a warning that while it could grant three wishes it would do so, "to their sorrow." They wish for a sum of money sufficient to settle their mortgage and receive that exact amount in settlement after their son is killed in a horrible industrial accident.

Publishing yourself looks easy—and glamorous—when you watch the e-book superstars laughing all the way to the bank. The reality for the vast majority of people who release their own work is at best unremarkable and often disappointing.

Part of the reason is simply structural: much of our social and economic world is governed by a power law distribution, where a few elements—be they cities, celebrities, or songs—stand out by orders of magnitude from their peers. Some things, for reasons beyond anyone's control, become runaway social phenomena. But those blockbusters are always the exception, not the rule.

A more important reason—because it is a matter over which you have some control—that many people are disappointed with the results of their efforts at self-publishing stems from the weight of expectations they bring along with them.

The electronic pioneers help inflate expectations because their experience comes from a time when demand exceeded supply. But the deeper and more pervasive problem is something akin to the gamblers fallacy: you believe that you will be the exception—that even though sales of most books are best measured in hundreds of copies, your book is going to sell tens or even hundreds of thousands of copies.

But the deepest reason many people find the path of the artisan disappointing is because they didn't understand what they were signing up for. Beyond straightforward matters like the quality and integrity of your product, you make a commitment to your readers when you publish something. The nature of the commitment is nebulous—you generally have no further customer obligations after someone purchases your book—but it is real enough that businesses account for it under the heading goodwill. If you want your books to continue to sell, you have to continue to market your books. You have to periodically release new material in order to be a publisher. Continuing to show up in the marketplace reassures your readers that they have bought into a going concern. If you, "fire and forget," a few books, readers will return the favor.

Artisan publishing is not something to be undertaken on a whim, but in the full and sober knowledge that you may be setting out on a long, difficult road that will yield success slowly at best.

TWO ROADS DIVERGED IN A YELLOW WOOD

I have been haunted by Robert Frost's, "The Road Not Taken," [8] ever since I blundered into the poem during a high school English class. The final stanza should be familiar:

> I shall be telling this with a sigh
> Somewhere ages and ages hence:
> Two Roads diverged in a wood, and I—
> I took the one less traveled by,
> And that has made all the difference.

Is this a lament or an expression of quiet gratitude about the road not taken?

The notion of opportunity costs is a poorly understood economic concept for similar reasons. As part of an effort to quantify what it will cost to pursue some line of endeavor you should add in the cost of not doing something else. In the relatively simple case of an investment, the opportunity cost of buying stock is the interest you would have earned if you left the money in the bank. The analysis, however, rapidly becomes much more complicated as you move from the predictable to the unpredictable. For example, what is the opportunity cost of taking one job instead of another, or marrying one person instead of another?

Artisan publishing doesn't preclude other kinds of publishing. There are certainly cases where an artisan publishing effort led to a lucrative contract with a major publisher. But a simple fact of life is that the more time you put in to one line of endeavor, the less time you have for others.

In the third stanza, Frost says:

And both that morning equally lay
In leaves no step had trodden black.
Oh, I kept the first for another day!
Yet knowing how way leads on to way,
I doubted if I should ever come back.

Your good intentions notwithstanding, way inevitably leads on to way and the road of artisan publishing will take you to different places than the well-marked path of traditional publishing.

It isn't simply that in addition to writing you will have to become skilled at production and marketing, it's that as an artisan publisher the nature of the projects you undertake will be different: you may choose to publish a manuscript that agents and editors say isn't sufficiently commercial; you may produce a collection of short stories or a novella that would have stood little chance of being published in the past because it was too long for a magazine and too short for a book; or you may simply write more or less than a traditional publisher is willing to absorb.

The differences arise not because one road is better than another but because they simply go to different places. What counts as success for an artisan is different from what counts as success for a large organization. Making money is, of course, part of both roads, but questions of how and why have different answers depending on the road.

If, instead of being fascinated with the new prospects that open up as you go down the road, you find yourself looking over your shoulder and spending more time wondering about the other road—the one more traveled by, and better marked—then perhaps artisan publishing is not for you.

CHAPTER 36.

THE ADVANTAGES OF BEING AN ARTISAN PUBLISHER

Though you may have your doubts after the last chapter, artisan publishing can be a deeply rewarding vocation if you have the right temperament, attitude, and expectations. While advantages like editorial control and a faster publication schedule are obvious, the real advantages of the publishing road not taken are more subtle—and more significant.

IT'S NOT JUST A JOB

Listening to a group of multi-published, professional authors, the conversation, which touched on story structure and techniques of characterization, was interesting but the offhand way in which they referred to their various books when illustrating a point sounded cavalier. Later, while discussing a project with a roofing contractor, I heard the same tone as he talked about the jobs he'd done. Then I recognized what had bothered me about the authors' conversation: they gave me the impression that their writing had become just a series of jobs.

"Wait," you say, "why is that a bad thing? I'm reading this book because I want writing to be my job."

There's an important difference between making a living from your writing and letting your writing become a job or, worse, thinking of stories as simply products.

I took a seminar on professional academic writing in graduate school. Toward the end of semester, the professor outlined the schedule of papers and books we needed to publish if we wanted to advance through the academic ranks and ultimately receive tenure. I had enjoyed the class up to that point, but the notion of writing to a schedule—whether or not I had something to say—seemed wrong.

It's not that I was surprised to learn that one does a tremendous amount of writing as a professor, it's that I naïvely believed academic writing was motivated by having information to share and not simply a selfish need to produce a mass of manuscripts sufficient to tip the tenure committee's scales.

Readers value the emotional experience of reading a book. The only sure way to capture an authentic emotional experience in prose is to feel it as you write. It's hard to feel the full range of the emotions if the story you're writing is just another job to help pay the bills. In contrast, if your story means something more to you than fulfilling a contractual obligation or a potential financial return, it's hard not to feel the full range of emotions.

Artisan publishing is a terrible get-rich-quick scheme. That may sound like a liability but it is actually an asset. Without the pressure created by the possibility of making a fast buck, you are free to write and publish because it's meaningful to you—because you have something you want to contribute to the great cultural conversation and the story is worth sharing.

Of course artisan publishing is a business and you must never forget sound business principles. But artisan publishing is a small business. Large businesses like corporations with shareholders must always try to maximize their financial return. Private businesses can define success differently. One of the perks of owning a small business is that you can say no to a job—or say yes to a job that may not make you a lot of money but is good business for other reasons.

FREED FROM THE BED OF PROCRUSTES

Theseus, the mythical founder-king of Athens, defeated a series of bandits when he traveled from Troezen to Athens to claim his birthright. The last of these was Procrustes, a hospitable fellow with an obsessive compulsion to make travelers fit his bed by lengthening or shortening them—which always proved fatal. Theseus took care of Procrustes by giving him a taste of his own hospitality.

Condemning trade publishers by associating them with Procrustes is unnecessarily hyperbolic. Nevertheless, there is some truth in the observation that publishers only want projects that fit certain parameters. Just like movie theaters, which are designed to make money with movies running between ninety and hundred and twenty minutes and thus have a hard time accommodating significantly longer or shorter films, book buyers expect their physical copies to have a certain heft after they've parted with fifteen to twenty-five dollars and everyone wants a spine wide enough to accommodate a readable title. This is why the sweet spot for novel length lies between 60,000 and 90,000 words.

A funny thing happened when books became digital. While physicists assure us electrons have mass, your average reader can't tell the difference in the heft of their e-reading device of choice between 50,000 word and 500,000 word books. Books no longer must be a certain size in order to fit the requirements of bookstores. Put another way, the value readers derive from a book is now primarily a function of its content, not its form.

Readers, of course, still have expectations, which you ignore at your peril. But compared to the previously established order, you now have far more latitude in the size and scope of the projects you publish.

BACK TO THE FUTURE

What's ironic, if you expand your scope from the past seventy-five years to the half–millennium since Gutenberg's revolution in printing, is that artisan publishing is actually more traditional than *traditional* publishing. Many of the exciting new possibilities, like selling monthly installments of a larger work or crowdsourcing the capital to produce a book, were used more than a century ago by obscure writers like Charles Dickens and Mark Twain.

We are now free to try other, more traditional publishing models. In some cases, we may fail because the model is flawed. In other cases, we may discover models that failed in the past are now viable.

Artisan publishing allows us to get past trade publishers to the real traditions of publishing and abolish the notion of one true publishing model.

MARCH TO THE BEAT OF YOUR OWN DRUMMER

Most of the timetables of trade publishers—retail seasons, book launches, and publishing one book a year from an author—have nothing to do with the needs of readers and writers, and everything to do with the needs of publishers and booksellers.

A remarkable, and liberating, thing happens when you follow the artisan path: all of the timetables we associate with publishing change and most of them become irrelevant. When you are writing and publishing books that will be on sale for decades, you don't have to worry about retail seasons: if you miss one season your book will be ready for the next, and from the perspective of a decade a twelve month delay won't make much of a difference. Book launches can be fun but they aren't necessary because readers no longer have only three or four months to find your book on the shelves. And you can clearly publish as fast—or as slow—as you want.

But it's even better than that. If something comes up that requires a change of plans, you're the only one affected. Yes, it might mean another year or two before you can quit your day job, but the sun will continue to rise and set on the literary world with or without your contributions. This doesn't mean your contributions are meaningless, rather it means that you are free from the oppression (and consequent depression) of external timetables and can devote the energy freed up by not having to worry about such things to producing your own work according to your own timetable.

PUBLISHING AS A PROCESS, NOT AN EVENT

One of the advantages artisan publishers enjoy is that

they can treat the publication of a title has an ongoing process, unlike their traditional brethren for whom publishing a title is an event. Artisan publishers can choose to invest more in titles that are doing well—perhaps in the form of new cover, a new edition, or a follow-on volume.

When investing more, artisan publishers would do well to follow the example of venture capitalists, who regularly review their portfolios and walk away from companies that are doing poorly in order to cut their losses, let the companies that are going to break even produce a return, and pump more money into the clear winners.

There is, of course, a limit to what you can accomplish for a book by simply putting more money into it. No amount of additional investment will make every book a bestseller. Instead, as an artisan publisher, you're looking to see which books resonate best with your readers because those indicate where you should focus your new efforts. If, for example, you thought of yourself as a writer of important literary fiction and find that readers are buying your humorous essays at a ratio of ten to one, perhaps you should set aside your literary ambitions and give your readers more of what they want.

YOU CAN ALWAYS QUIT

As important as it is to dabble privately and only publish if you are willing to devote yourself to the long, quiet path of the artist and craftsman, one of the biggest, and frankly most liberating, advantages of choosing artisan publishing over any of the partnerships that fall under the heading of traditional publishing is that you can always quit.

Yuvi Zalkow explained how the option of quitting is actually empowering:

"When I was going through one of my first major bouts of depression ten years ago and my therapist was strongly suggesting anti-depressant medication ... I went back and forth with my therapist until she said something pretty simple: You know, if you don't like it, you can always quit.... Sticking with a difficult project today doesn't mean you're stuck with it tomorrow. Are you up for working on it today?" [9]

When you sign a contract, you accept a legal obligation to deliver what you have promised. Contracts usually include a termination clause, which spells out the consideration due the other party (i.e., the penalty you'll pay) if you can't uphold your end of the deal. The practical upshot of entering into a traditional arrangement with a publishing partner is that quitting is hard.

As both author and publisher, you're not under any obligation to write or release any project: remember, no one asked you to do this. You retain the option to abandon or postpone your work. Yes, you will have to bear the sunk costs of the efforts already invested, but that is a risk with any project. And even if you do everything right, once you release your lovingly crafted book it will be subject to the whims of the marketplace.

As with social contracts in general, when you enter into a publishing partnership you trade some autonomy for the benefits provided by the other party. Self–publishing is often characterized as a way to maintain creative control. We usually think of *creative control* in terms of how we create. But the full scope of creative control includes the choice of whether or not to create.

* * *

The biggest advantage of being an artisan publisher, which is also the biggest challenge in becoming as an artisan publisher, is creative or editorial control—a topic that deserves a chapter of its own.

CHAPTER 37.

EDITORIAL CONTROL

Professional editing is high on the list of indispensable things traditional publishers claim to provide authors. And they are right when they say every project should receive a professional edit before being published. But disingenuous, at best, to claim they are the only ones who can provide it.

Professional editing has two key aspects: coherence and vision—both of which you need to master as an artisan publisher.

COHERENCE, QUALITY, AND INTEGRITY

Coherence covers what most of us think of when we say editing: everything from the developmental edit, which focuses on the logic and consistency of the plot and the believability of the characters, to the copy edit, which gets into the nitty-gritty of grammar and usage. You may think of this kind of editing as fundamentally about improving the quality and integrity of your book. Quality and integrity are, however, facets of a deeper question: do the words you've written make enough sense to another person that they will enjoy reading your book and feel satisfied it was worth the asking price?

You can never fully answer that question yourself because you know what the words are supposed to mean. Whether you use beta readers or hire an editor, it's critical to get your work in front of other people and see how they react to it before you publish.

What you can and should do is become as proficient as possible in writing and editing so that your editor or beta reader can spend his or her time focusing on story and character instead of getting hung up on mechanical problems you could have caught and corrected. Not only will you save in editorial charges, the work they deliver will provide greater value to you because it will focus on things you can't see or fix by yourself.

The vision a professional editor can provide is a more subtle but ultimately more valuable contribution to the success of the finished book. The relationship between an editor and an author in the traditional publishing system is somewhat like the relationship between the producer and the director in the movie industry: in broad strokes, the director is responsible for the dramatic content and its artistic integrity and the producer is responsible for the package that will be distributed and presented to viewers. Similarly, the author is responsible for the manuscript and the editor is responsible for turning the manuscript into a book that entices readers to buy.

As an artisan publisher, the responsibility to have and follow through on a vision of how your manuscript can become a book in the market falls squarely on your shoulders. You still need an outside editor, but they have no incentive to worry about the long-term prospects of the book because they're getting paid to do a short term job. Staff editors at traditional publishers act more like producers because they need a string of successful books to build their careers. When you follow the path of artisan publishing, you are the company and no one else has as much invested in the success of your books as you do.

You may be tempted to think of production simply in terms of a good cover, promotional copy, metadata, file formats, and uploading procedures. Doing so starts you down the road toward shotgun salesmanship—if you put out enough stuff someone's bound to find something they like. A professional editor's production role is about precision and authority: it is the heart of the gatekeeping about which we so dearly love to complain. Professional editors curate submitted manuscripts, selecting only the best to offer to the public. Your goal as an artisan publisher is similar: every book you release should be one you truly believe is worth a reader's time and attention—not because doing so serves some nebulous, greater cultural good but because it is the single most effective way to build your business.

DEVELOPING YOUR EDITORIAL VISION

A professional editor's vision for a book depends upon a mixture of instinct and skill. Your instincts about what your book could be and how it might find a place in the market are best developed by paying attention, especially to your readers. Calling it *market research* is offputtingly-formal because it's simply a matter of doing what you've likely been doing all along: reading books, paying attention to what others are reading, and keeping an eye on what seems to be attracting attention in the market.

You don't need to track the week-by-week progress of every new release. You simply need to be aware enough of your readers to avoid offering something they can ignore because it's either derivative or impenetrable. In other words, the essence of your editorial vision is seeing how to bring something new to the conversation.

As with writing in general, vision is necessary but not sufficient: it doesn't matter how vividly you perceive the possibilities for your book if you can't express them clearly and concisely. The best way to express your vision is by answering the basic who-what-where-and-why questions people will have when they hear about a new project:

- Who is the audience?
- What does this book give the audience that they need or want?
- Where are potential readers going to find this book?
- Why, with all the other distractions in their lives, should people pay attention to this book?

Once you've developed your vision of the place your book could have in the world, you must shepherd it through the production process. Your editorial vision guides you through the thousand-and-one choices to be made about covers and copy and marketing so that all the disparate elements come together in a cohesive package designed to give your book the best possible shot at achieving its potential.

Editorial vision is one area where, as an artisan publisher, you're likely to do either substantially better or worse than an editor at a traditional publisher. On one hand, you love your story more than a staff editor, who has to do the same job with at least a dozen other manuscripts each year and can't afford to add the extra touches that will extend your book's appeal to smaller, more specialized markets. On the other, your infatuation can blind you to market realities and your unrealistic expectations can lure you across the line between vision and delusion. Envisioning a book whose quality matches or surpasses anything coming out of New York can drive your project to new heights. Envisioning the cast for the inevitable movie that will be made from your book can drive you mad with frustration.

SELF-EDITING FOR FUN AND PROFIT

The basic problem with self-editing—that it is much easier to spot other's faults—is a general human failing memorialized in the wisdom literature of many cultures. The **New Testament**, for example, describes the hypocrisy of offering to help a neighbor pluck a mote (a dust speck) from their eye while ignoring the beam (something much larger) in your own.

When it comes to self-editing, we are all hypocrites because we know what our words are supposed to mean. The fact that the editor you engage is another person is the single most important reason for engaging them: ignorant of what you intended when you wrote the words, they can only work with the words you put on the page.

That said, even if you hire one or more editors, final editorial responsibility rests with you because you are the one who must determine when a project is finished.

In order to be an effective editor, you need two brains: a reader brain that has never seen the text before, and an author brain that knows the intent of each passage and scene. It's not enough to simply flag a problem; you also need a sense of which of the many ways of solving the problem best supports the larger purpose of the book. In other words, you need to cultivate a perspective that enables you to see both forest and trees.

The two best ways to gain perspective are:

1. Find people who are willing to read and provide feedback on your project.
2. Set your project aside and focus on something else for at least a month.

After you've gained the perspective afforded by time and distance you're ready to begin critical editing. Overall your strategy should be to move from breadth to depth: you don't want to spend time perfecting a scene only to decide later that it doesn't belong in the story at all.

Start with a big-picture read and look at the overall logic, pacing, and emotional resonance of your story. Try to read the entire book in one or a few sittings. It's often helpful to change the medium—if, for example, you drafted the book with a word processor, now would be a good time to print out a full copy. Because your goal is to get a sense of the overall flow of the story, flag any problems you find with a quick mark but don't take time to consider how they may be fixed.

Once you're satisfied with the story as a whole—that you've eliminated unnecessary scenes, added missing scenes, and arranged them all in the proper order—it's time for a second pass to assess the effectiveness of each scene. This is where you concentrate on showing character development, both within and across scenes. Are your characters consistent? Are their motivations clear? Is there anything missing from the scene? Is there anything in the scene that should be cut because it doesn't help move the story forward?

The final editing pass is devoted to details: typos, grammar, and awkward phrasing. Reading the work aloud is a particularly effective way to catch problems. This is also the time to verify details and check continuity. For example, are there unmotivated changes in characters' physical attributes?

As for the actual process of making editorial changes, you can save yourself lots of grief by making a copy of your document and using your word processor's track changes feature. It's often helpful to ease into the process of reworking the document you thought was finished a month ago by starting with the easy changes: correcting typos, fixing continuity mistakes, and straightening out awkward sentences. As the number of minor changes accumulates, the prospect of major changes becomes less daunting.

The process of refining a manuscript until it is ready for publication is not a trivial one. Whether you engage an editor or, in conjunction with outside readers, do most of the editing yourself, you should expect the process to take two to three times as long as it took to compose the first draft.

Editing is a topic to which many good books have been devoted. [10] As part of your preparations to become an artisan publisher, you should acquire and study several of them.

STYLE SHEETS

Style sheets are the secret tool of professional editors.

With a bold introduction like that, you may be disappointed to learn that a style sheet is nothing more than a list of editorial decisions to which you can refer when you come upon another instance of an issue in the manuscript so that you handle them consistently. Everything from proper names (particularly if they have an unusual spelling) and character attributes (hair color, a limp, speaking in a dialect, etc.) to matters of grammar and punctuation (like preferring the Oxford or serial comma). You'll save yourself trouble, and increase your confidence, if you compile your style sheet as you write.

The power of style sheets goes well beyond editing your manuscript. You'll have to master a large set of tools as you take your project from concept to finished book, but many of the steps are ones you'll only do occasionally. With so much to keep track of, how can you avoid becoming a jack of all trades and master of none?

The trick is to write down everything in your process style sheet so that you can save yourself the trouble of relearning things the second time around. Assume your reader knows nothing about the process when you write down the steps. And don't give into the temptation to skip the parts that seem obvious, because when you come back months or years later it won't be obvious.

Yes, it is tedious to write everything down. And yes, it will slow you down. But nothing is as frustrating as discovering a task you thought you could handle in a reasonable amount of time is going to take significantly longer because you forgot how to do it.

CHAPTER 38.

THE CHALLENGES OF ARTISAN PUBLISHING

We call careers and lifestyles where the boring bits escape (or are hidden from) our notice glamorous. It is only when we try to follow the path in earnest that we discover it's not all wine and roses. Artisan publishing is no different: the way is fraught with unexpected challenges.

THE PRICE OF FREEDOM

Independence is a funny thing: when we celebrate the independence of the United States from Great Britain we hear a lot about freedom but not so much about responsibility. The standard narrative often runs along the lines of, "Things were difficult in 1776 but the founding fathers were men of vision and courage—and look where we are today." We conveniently gloss over the first hundred years of the country's history when its viability—and sometimes its existence—were often in doubt.

The standard narrative about independent publishing is similar: heavy on the new-found freedoms authors enjoy but light on the new responsibilities they must shoulder.

Like investments, where greater rewards are always accompanied by greater risks, independence is a consistently harder road than dependence because taking responsibility is the price of admission. One of the comforts in the old way of publishing was there were enough people involved that you could exempt yourself if you needed to place blame: the publisher chose a bad cover, the sales force failed to promote the book, or some event distracted the public. The inescapable truth of independent publishing is that the book with your name on it is no one's fault but your own.

You may think taking full responsibility for your book sounds harsh and that you don't have to go it alone. There is nothing wrong with finding partners for your publishing project, but even then you are still responsible for making sure they are the right partners and that they do the job properly.

WHEN IS IT DONE?

Another under-appreciated luxury built in to traditional publishing arrangements is that someone else decides when the book is finished and ready to be released.

"Wait," you may say, raising an eyebrow, "isn't one of the biggest advantages of artisan publishing by-passing the gatekeepers? And now you're saying the gatekeepers are a good thing?"

Thanks to pop psychology, we often associate a need for validation with a weakness of character. But the essence of the scientific method is to seek external validation: having an independent party confirm your claims begins to move the proposition from the murk of subjectivity into the light of objectivity. Compared to science, literature is hopelessly subjective—the list of books we call classics, for example, is purely a matter of consensus and always changes over time. We have no objective criteria for determining how good a book is or how well it will do in the market. Instead, we put our faith in the authority and judgment of people like editors and publishers who have experience in the industry.

The value of having someone else decide when the project is ready goes beyond validation. We are much more willing to believe a third party who says the work is good than we are to believe the author, who is tainted by self-interest. Beyond social conventions, there's the very real problem of confusing forests and trees: we are rightly suspicious of people who declare their own work to be good because of the risk that they have lost perspective. This is why it's critical to get a second pair of eyes on your project.

The problem you face as an artisan publisher, particularly if it is your own work you will be publishing, is that it is your inescapable responsibility to decide when the work is finished. Of course you can engage editors and reviewers, but you still have to decide when to stop incorporating feedback and release the work.

There is no formula that will tell you when your book is ready. It's a matter of taste and instinct. And there is not shortcut for developing either taste or instinct. You must dissect other projects, studying their constituent elements and judging how finished each one feels.

GETTING BORED WITH YOURSELF

One of the critical steps in the hero's journey is the point at which the would-be hero meets his mentor. The mentor may provide shelter, training, and encouragement at a critical time when the hero is on the verge of giving up his quest, but more important than any one of those things is the perspective the mentor—who has actually been down the road before—provides.

Counselors say many people who come to see them know what they should do but need someone to help them recognize what they already know and, perhaps more importantly, give them permission to do it. As much as we may not want to admit it, we all require external validation. We find it difficult to break out of the cycle of self-doubt without it. In the hero's journey the final service the mentor performs is to tell the hero he or she is ready. The hero may not believe in themselves yet, but they continue their journey because they trust their mentor.

Losing perspective is a constant risk for artisan publishers.

An obvious example is convincing yourself the project is finished when it isn't. This loss of perspective is generally the result of inexperience or hubris. The best antidote is to read widely to develop a sense of the level of quality the market expects and to refine your own taste.

A more subtle loss of perspective occurs when you've grown bored—or sick—of your project. When you just want to be done so you can move on to something else, it's difficult to resist the temptation to publish too soon. Your best recourse, if you recognize your mood deteriorating, is to step away from the project.

As the final decision-maker, you've got to work at least twice as hard to maintain your standards of quality.

NUMBERS AND RANKINGS

As much as we like to believe we're superior to other species, the fact of the matter is that we are primates. One of the consequences of being a primate is that a large portion of our monkey brain is devoted to tracking status and social rank. Robert M. Sapolsky, writing in **Scientific American**, explains it this way:

> "... across the primate species, the percentage of the brain devoted to the neocortex correlates with the average size of the social group of that species. This correlation is more dramatic in humans ... than in any other primate species. In other words, the most distinctively primate part of the human brain coevolved with the demands of keeping track of who is not getting along with whom, who is tanking in the dominance hierarchy and what couple is furtively messing around when they should not be." [11]

It's no accident social media systems include some sort of follower count because we can't resist the urge to improve our social ranking. Whether or not it really matters—and with current social media one suspects that ultimately it doesn't—our brains are wired to trigger reward circuits whenever we do something that increases our perceived social status.

More generally, we feel compelled to optimize the numbers we track. That's why sales figures and sales rankings are dangerous. It's easy to get trapped in a spiral of trying to improve your numbers and then getting depressed because other people are doing better than you.

Beyond their effect on your mental health, sales numbers and rankings are bad for business. Rankings distract you from what you're trying to build as an artisan publisher.

And what are you trying to build?

A steady royalty stream.

If the only way you can sell books is through stunts, promotions, and constant fiddling with the price, cover, promotional copy, and so on, you don't have a sustainable business—because the minute you stop your mad dance, the sales stop too.

Your goal as an artisan publisher is to establish the business equivalent of the autonomous systems in your body: your heart pumps steadily, day and night, with little or no thought on your part. That's why it's important to understand the distinction between sales and marketing: sales is about asking people to buy your book now; marketing is about helping people find your book when they are looking for something like it.

This is not to say that all you have to do is throw your book into the market and then sit back and watch the money roll in. A book can't sell if no one knows about it. Marketing is the way you prime the pump, but a sustainable project needs to sell beyond the circle of people you can influence directly.

Above all, no matter how seductive the numbers may be, if you want to be an artisan publisher you must never let them distract you from your core job of writing great books.

EMBARRASSMENT OF RICHES

Dr. Stephen Goldbart, a licensed clinical psychologist, has made a career of helping people suffering from what he calls Sudden Wealth Syndrome or SWS. Comedians, naturally, have had a field day with SWS, joking that it's a syndrome we'd all like to catch.

As with many things, even ones that seem silly or self-indulgent, there's usually a kernel of truth at the core. People who win lotteries, receive a substantial inheritance, or sell a business at a handsome profit often, after an initial binge of spending, find themselves feeling guilty, isolated, and depressed. The fundamental problem is that they don't know what to do with themselves or with their newfound fortune.

The difference between right and wrong is usually clear in the stories we tell our children. As they mature, young people are able to handle a greater degree of moral ambiguity and they begin to grapple with the question of how to decide what to do when the right course of action isn't obvious. A variation on that question, which continues to challenge us as adults, is how to decide among options that are all demonstrably good.

Sudden wealth syndrome is a special case of the general problem of deciding among many good options. Much of the stress suffered by the suddenly wealthy comes from well-meaning people offering suggestions about the best way to use the new fortune. The flood of possibilities proves overwhelming without an organizing framework.

Artisan publishers suffer from a similar, albeit far less dramatic, embarrassment of riches because there are many good ways you could use your time to further your enterprise: there's always room for more editorial polish on the works currently in progress; you probably have a long list of new projects; on the production side, perhaps you should enrich the back matter, experiment with different titles and covers, or take a course to improve your skills in graphic design and layout; and, because you can never do enough marketing, maybe you should launch a strategic ad campaign, organize a blog tour, solicit reviews, or expand your social network.

One of the fundamental principles of artisan publishing is that we will release a project only when it meets our standards of craft and quality, and not simply because of an arbitrary schedule. But there's a subtle danger in this commitment to the integrity of the work: of the many good things you could do to improve the quality of the work, how do you decide what to do, what not to do, and when the work is done?

The answer for the suddenly wealthy is to slow down and rethink their value system, identifying what matters and those things that are truly important. For the artisan publisher, the answer begins with the realization that they can never please everybody and that the essence of craftsmanship is to do the work to their own satisfaction: the master, unlike the journeyman or apprentice, knows when the work is good enough.

CHAPTER 39.

GRAPPLING WITH THE TIME BEAST

In J.R.R. Tolkien's **The Hobbit**, Gollum asks the following riddle:

> This thing all things devours:
> Birds, beasts, trees, flowers;
> Gnaws iron, bites steel;
> Grinds hard stones to meal;
> Slays kings, ruins town,
> And beats high mountain down.

Bilbo is flummoxed and begs for time, which is the answer.

Like the inexorable force in Gollum's riddle, time can wear away your enthusiasm, resolve, and (ultimately) will—unless you understand the nature of the beast and set your expectations accordingly.

IDEAL TIME AND REAL TIME

In an episode of **Star Trek: The Next Generation**, titled, "Relics," the crew of the Enterprise-D find Scotty, the chief engineer from the original Enterprise, trapped in the transporter buffer. Scotty later has an opportunity to give Geordi La Forge, chief engineer on the Enterprise-D, a lesson in old-school engineering:

> "I told the Captain I would have this diagnostic done in an hour."
> "And how long will it really take you?"
> "An hour!"
> "Oh, you didn't tell him how long it would really take, did you?"
> "Of course I did."
> "Oh, laddie, you have a lot to learn if you want people to think of you as a miracle worker."
> —La Forge and Scotty

Engineers have a grand tradition of inflating estimates. Although it sounds self-serving, the practice is grounded on sound engineering principles. Most people, when asked to estimate how long it will take to complete a job, give a best-case estimate. They tend to assume nothing will go wrong and everything will work as expected because of the deep-seated desire to please we all share.

However, engineers understand a great truth: the difference between theory and practice is that in theory there is no difference. In all but the most trivial projects something inevitably goes wrong, people get sidetracked, or there's a surprise. Good engineers routinely take their estimate and double or triple it to account for the unexpected.

Artisan publishing is very much like engineering in that you've entered into a new relationship with time—one in which everything will take longer than you expect.

You may object that one of the much touted advantages of publishing yourself is that you're not bound by the maddening delays inherent in the publishing industry. Besides, small organizations are supposed to be more nimble than large ones. As a publishing organization comprised of yourself and perhaps a few others you're definitely small, so you should be faster, right?

First, assuming you're committed to producing works of comparable quality, publishing yourself is faster than working with a traditional publisher only if you have a manuscript that's ready to be published when you decide to publish. Regardless of how you publish, it will still take you the same amount of time to write and revise each book. While it may take less calendar time for you to go from finished manuscript to released book, you will be spending time preparing your book for publication that you won't be able to spend writing another book. The bottom line is that books worth reading take time to produce—more than you think.

Second, if you're like most people, your estimates are based on ideal writing hours. Splitting the 168 hours allotted to each week among sleep, family, work, community, and your writing, means there aren't that many hours to allocate to writing in the first place. And of those hours, which will be interspersed among other necessary activities, you'll spend a fair number of them coming back up to speed every time you sit down to write. In other words, your estimates of how long it will take to write a given project probably don't to take into account the time required to shift mental contexts from other tasks to your writing. As long as you're not devoting your full-time efforts to your publishing enterprise your project time frames are best measured in months if not years.

One of the realities of commercial publishing is that you spend a lot of time waiting for people to read and act on your project. While patience is the single most important virtue you can cultivate as a writer, it's a requirement for artisan publishers.

The good news is that you get to set your own schedule, so if you miss your estimate you can simply revise your schedule.

THE 4X FACTOR

Project management depends upon good estimates. By knowing how long each task will take and which tasks depend upon others, you can sequence the work so that materials and subassemblies are delivered when needed and the project can be completed in the shortest possible calendar time. Unfortunately, as you move away from concrete tasks, like pouring footings and a slab, toward more abstract tasks, like writing and publishing the next great American novel, estimating the amount of time required becomes significantly more difficult.

Abstract tasks are difficult to estimate because it's hard to say how they should be done—or even when they are done. Concrete tasks have well-understood processes and specifications. We know which steps are required to produce a particular outcome and we know how long those steps take because we timed them on earlier jobs. Designing a cover for your book could take a day if you get it right the first time or months if you have to go through a hundred different concepts.

The situation, however, is worse for artisan publishers:

tasks are going to take an average of four times longer than you think they should.

FINDING TIME

To begin with, most artisan publishers will be working part-time—usually on evenings and weekends around a regular, full-time job. You may think that if you put in two hours a night on weeknights and ten hours each on Saturday and Sunday you will have thirty hours a week. But even if you have no other people, interests, errands, or emergencies intruding upon those hours you won't be able to sustain your creativity and you may not even be able to keep up with your responsibilities at work without some down time. Fifteen hours a week—twenty tops—is realistically the amount of time you'll be able to devote to artisan publishing if your life includes significant others and a bit of leisure. So simply in terms of calendar time, your artisan publishing projects will take at least twice as long as a comparable project for your day job.

However, you will consistently underestimate your artisan publishing projects if you simply double the amount of time you think it should take because other factors like context switching, less concentrated time, and rusty tools conspire to slow you down by roughly another factor of two.

THE CONCEPTUAL CONTEXT

Unlike manual work, whose state is maintained by the workbench so that you can easily return to the task after an interruption, knowledge work happens primarily inside your head where an interruption sweeps away all your conceptual scaffolding by forcing you to pay attention to something else. Imagine having to clear everything off your workbench to answer the telephone and then set up your tools, the jig, and the work piece again before restarting the task. Studies have shown that programmers need half an hour to recover from a nontrivial interruption. Even if you can avoid interruptions during the time you're able to devote to artisan publishing projects you still need to switch gears from your day job and other concerns and reestablish the mental context for your writing and publishing tasks. If you need half an hour to get up to speed you'll spend about four of your fifteen to twenty hours a week in a less than fully productive mode.

CONCENTRATION TIME

Economies of scale allow many businesses to be profitable: the larger the production volume the smaller the per-unit cost and the higher the per-unit profit margin. Concentration time is the temporal analogue of economies of scale. As you concentrate on a task, you find ways to be more efficient. The pace at which you work goes up as you repeat a task: your confidence increases and you spend less time double-checking your work. And with writing, you can get into a zone where you stop tripping over words and sentences and instead see the action and hear the dialog. Day jobs commonly have periods of concentration time each morning and afternoon, where the second is a bit easier to resume. While you may be able to enjoy similar sets of concentration time on the weekend, week night concentration time is usually limited and often more likely to be interrupted. Less concentration time means less efficiency and slower progress on the project.

SERIAL SPECIALIZATION

Another, more subtle difference between full and part-time work is the working knowledge you develop of your toolset. Full-time work generally involves some degree of specialization, which means once you've learned how to use your tools you can jump right into subsequent projects without any additional training. Artisan publishing requires serial specialization, which means that your estimates need to include time to relearn tools you haven't used recently. The frustration of diving into a task you've done before only to discover you've forgotten the details can destroy your forward momentum if you're not prepared for this particularly insidious brand of project friction.

* * *

Taken all together, the realities of working evenings and weekends mean that an artisan publishing project will generally take four times as long on the calendar as a similar project for your day job. The total number of hours required by the project will also be larger, though the ratio is in the neighborhood of three to two (i.e., a forty-hour project at work will likely take 50 to 60 hours of evening and weekend time).

Of course, all of this changes if artisan publishing becomes your day job. But until you can afford to devote all your time to writing and publishing you need to accept the fact that nothing will happen as quickly as you would like.

DON'T PANIC (AND DON'T RUSH)

One of the most annoying business rationales is the *window of opportunity*, where a pot of gold is waiting if you can get your product to market in what's usually a ridiculously short time, otherwise conditions will change—competitors will enter the market, laws will go into effect, or the holiday will pass—and you'll be laughed to scorn by customers and competitors. The problem with windows of opportunity is that the situation is never as black and white as the executives paint it: the opportunity rarely disappears at the end of the window and new opportunities regularly arise. The only thing the window of opportunity does is create a heightened sense of urgency, making the effort more likely to prove the aphorism that haste makes waste.

Yes, there are times and seasons. Markets, particularly mass markets, have lifecycles: if one company gets to market first and saturates it, they effectively shut out competition. Demand for products clearly changes over time. Now that the age of the automobile is upon us, it would be foolhardy to set up a factory to produce a million buggy whips a month. But it's important to point out that to the demand for new buggy whips has not dropped to zero (even outside Amish communities).

Where books are concerned, some topics are clearly more timely than others. A shocking exposé of a seventeenth century monarch probably won't attract as many readers as would an exposé of a current political figure. A project about a historic event will likely garner more interest if its release coincides with the anniversary of that event.

However both projects will attract some readers

regardless of when they are published. So the real question is whether the projects will sell enough books to provide a return on the investment in a timely fashion. Trade publishers, for a variety of reasons, define timely return on the order of months. Artisan publishers, who are playing a different game, have the luxury of defining timely return on the order of years.

CHAPTER 40.

MASTERING YOUR CRAFT

There are many areas of endeavor where you need to show you know the rules before you can be trusted to break them. While nowhere near as critical as a licensed profession like medicine, publishing is structurally similar because you're asking people to trust that you can do what you claim to be able to do.

In the days of craft guilds, an artisan began as an apprentice, graduated to a journeyman when he had learned basic skills, and became a master—and independent businessman—only after producing a masterpiece to prove he had actually mastered all the facets of his craft. We are well past the time when the only way to learn was by doing, and it is neither practical nor necessary to apprentice yourself to an established publisher in order to learn the business, but the prerequisites of skill and mastery still apply if you want to be an artisan publisher.

Fortunately many of the skills you need as an artisan publisher are the same ones you need to live and work in the modern world: you need to know how to use the technical tools of your trade, particularly computers and the Internet; you need to know how to organize your time and work effectively; and you need to be able to plan, finish, and promote your projects.

TOOLS: NOT ONLY HOW, BUT WHY

An artisan understands his or her tools and can use them well. As an artisan publisher, you must understand both your individual tools and their role in your publishing process. It's not that you have to personally master every tool involved in the process, but you must understand the process well enough to know which things you can and should do and which things you should engage other artisans to do.

Mastering individual tools means not only familiarity and practice, but understanding their intended use, theory of operation, and limitations. While it is true that one tool may often be used in the place of another, if you don't understand why the different tools were developed in the first place you have not yet achieved mastery. For example, word processors and page layout programs can both be used to put words on paper, but the way in which you use them and the relative ease or difficulty of accomplishing specific tasks are very different because each kind of program was designed to solve different problems. The novice may know how to use a tool, but the master knows why.

THE MYSTERY OF STYLES

An example of the distinction between master and novice is whether you use styles in your word processor. Many older writers suffer from the curse of the typewriter: they were taught to make the paper look right—it didn't matter, for example, if you used tab settings or were in the habit of hitting the space bar some number of times to begin the paragraph so long as the first word was properly indented.

We deal with things as wholes in the analog world of our every-day experience. In the digital world, everything is broken down into atomic parts. Classifying the parts and specifying their role in the whole enables us to build systems that seem to behave with greater intelligence. A book is composed of chapters, which in turn contain text. But even this simple example isn't that simple: the opening line of the first paragraph following a heading is customarily not indented while the first lines of all other paragraphs in the section are indented.

If you make everything look right on the screen using the basic editing tools provided by your favorite word processor you will have formatting problems when you create print book layouts and e-book files. If you use styles to identify different kinds of text like chapter headings, subheadings, the first paragraph, and standard paragraphs you'll find that formatting your manuscript is a straightforward process.

SUSPENSION OF DISBELIEF

The rules of writing distill down to things that help or hinder readers as they try to suspend their disbelief. The hallmark of good writing is that it allows readers to forget they're reading a story and immerse themselves in the experience it conjures. The hallmark of bad writing is that it never lets readers forget they're reading a story because the author's fingerprints are all over it.

Publishers have a similar challenge. There are a number

of things readers expect from a book if they're to believe it is a work of literature and not just a stack of papers (or batch of electrons) designed to separate them from their hard earned cash.

You may find this notion easier to understand if you think in terms of fit and finish. In many endeavors, the work is functionally complete well before it is finished. A chassis with an engine, transmission, wheels, and controls enables you to move from one place to another, but it's not a car until it's got a body, seating, windshields, cup holders, and all the other things drivers have come to expect.

Much of what follows falls under the heading of book design. Volumes have been written on this topic and you would be well advised to add a few of them to your library. Our purpose here is to characterize the range of issues you need to consider if you want to give your readers books that satisfy their expectations for a professionally published project.

CLARITY

Though it may seem obvious, the first and most fundamental reader expectation is that the text is clear. Words must be spelled correctly, sentences must be grammatical, and the ideas expressed by those sentences should form a coherent narrative. Beyond editorial clarity, the presentation of the text should be clear: margins, font size, and line spacing must be consistent and chosen so as to give the reader a pleasant, trouble–free reading experience. Fonts that are too small, lines that are too close together, or margins that are too thin can all mislead the reader's eye and make it difficult to follow the text.

NAVIGATION

Navigation aids like chapters and sections help the reader to know the scope of the work and how the material is organized. Just as text broken up into paragraphs is easier to read than a single, undifferentiated block of text on the page, a manuscript broken up into clearly identified chapters and sections is easier to commit to reading than a volume where pages run endlessly on without a break.

Different kinds of books, of course, require different levels of navigation. A reference or textbook may need both a thorough index and a table of contents outlining sections three or four levels deep. A novel may need nothing more than a list of chapters.

SUPPORTING MATERIAL

The difference between a book and manuscript is that the book is a package that provides a context for the manuscript. In addition to the main body text, a book should include whatever else a reader may require to get value from that text. Printed books generally place a copyright statement and information about the publisher, dedications and introductory material such as a preface or foreword, and a table of contents before the primary text. Notes, a bibliography, indexes, acknowledgments, and lists of related works available from the publisher generally follow the text.

There is no single standard for what should comprise the front and back matter of the book. But if you understand what is commonly done and choose the elements that best fit your project, your book will feel more finished.

COVERS AND PACKAGING

Notwithstanding clichéd admonitions to the contrary, we all judge books by their covers. Of course, what we're really judging is the context, not the content. We do it all the time. If we're shopping for real estate, for example, we judge a property by its neighborhood when choosing the houses we want to take the trouble of inspecting more closely.

A book's packaging—its cover, jacket text, descriptions, and metadata—sets the tone for the reader's initial experience with the book. An amateurish cover suggests amateurish contents. Mistakes in the cover copy likely mean the text is riddled with typos. A crisp, professional presentation, on the other hand, implies the same level of care throughout the book.

One critical difference between covers for physical and electronic books is that readers are likely to see the cover image for the latter first as a thumbnail. Instead of having the full print size of the book as a canvas, the cover design needs to work as a tiny compressed image. Cover design is an art, the full examination of which is beyond our scope, but a good rule of thumb for the thumbnail image is a design employing a single, strong image, with large, concise title text.

CHAPTER 41.

THE ARTISAN PHILOSOPHY OF BUSINESS

Authors have historically distanced themselves from commercial concerns. Even though their livelihoods depend on selling books, most writers who work with trade publishers indulge in a pleasant fiction that their business is art and culture, not tawdry commerce.

WRITERS ARE INDEPENDENT BUSINESS PEOPLE

Traditional authors' consistent aversion to business stems from a simple but important structural fact: aside from advances, they only got paid twice a year. Worse, the biannual royalty payments reflected the sales that occurred during the six-month accounting period that closed six months prior to the payment. In other words, by the time a writer received a royalty payment there was no way to know whether anything they had done to promote their books had materially affected their sales.

At a personal level, the standard royalty payment schedule encouraged writers to view money in terms of either feast or famine. That, coupled with the solitary nature of the writing life, made it far easier for authors to understand themselves and their income in the same terms as artists and grants, not as independent business people working on long-term contracts.

The game-changer for artisan publishers was the advent of distribution partners who pay monthly royalties. Thanks to far more transparent sales accounting systems, payments are made sixty days after the close of the accounting month. More importantly, electronic publishers can now track sales on a daily basis, making it possible to correlate them with marketing and promotional efforts.

There are a number of ways to use these new tools, no one of which is guaranteed to work all the time. What's critical to understand, however, is that regular income and the ability to monitor your sales makes the fact that writers are independent business people clear.

ECON 101

Being in business is very much like being part of an ecosystem. An economic entity takes inputs from suppliers, adds value by transforming the inputs, and delivers the resulting product or service to customers. If you're missing any of the three key elements—suppliers, a process that adds value, and customers—you're not in business.

Most of us participate in the economy as employees, which means we're in the business of trading our time and effort for money. We then use that money to purchase goods and services from our preferred suppliers. Economists characterize this activity as consumption because we don't use the goods or services to add value to our products (except perhaps in the abstract sense that they enable us to continue to trade our time and effort for money).

One way you know you're in business is when money starts flowing to you. Having a positive cash flow, however, is simply the natural effect of identifying and reaching the consumers (readers) for whom your product (your writing) adds enough value that they are willing to include you in their list of suppliers, and by so doing integrate you into their economic network.

What sets a business apart from other kinds of economic activity is the process of adding value. But value is ultimately subjective. We can only add value to the goods and services we obtain from our suppliers if we have customers willing to purchase our products at a price that yields a profit.

In the terms we've just discussed, writing may seem like a curious business. Your primary supplier is locked inside your skull and the principal raw material you consumed to produce your product is time. Structurally, your business has more in common with a resource extraction business like lumber or mining than a retail shop. Resource extraction industries generally produce commodities, which means they must compete on price and availability. One of the principal complaints of trade publishers is that electronic distribution has reduced books to commodities. The explosion of low-priced e-books lends credence to this complaint. But the technological changes that have made e-books possible have become the scapegoat for an inconvenient yet persistent truth about publishing: until readers know why they should care about a book, it is a commodity.

So the real key to being in business as an artisan publisher is to add enough value to your books that they ceased to be commodities and instead become products your readers demand.

GROWING YOUR BUSINESS

In his classic book, **Growing a Business**, Paul Hawken argues most businesses fail because, before they ran out of the money, they had too much. When you hear Hawken's argument your first inclination is to say he's wrong: businesses fail because they run out of money so how could they ever have too much? Hawkin's point is more subtle. Of course, businesses ultimately fail because they can no longer pay their bills. The reason they can no longer pay their bills, according to Hawken, is because in a well-funded startup there is much less urgency to make sure the business is self-sustaining. The seeds of eventual scarcity were sown by the initial abundance.

One of the most egregious ways in which well-funded businesses prepare themselves to fail is by investing a substantial portion of their startup capital into looking like a business: they rent high-profile office space and fill it with expensive office furniture in the belief that they'll get more business if they look like a going concern. But looking like a going concern and actually becoming one are very different things and in the long run a company that actually becomes a going concern will get much more business than one that only looked like it until the money ran out.

Don't rush to look like you're in business. Focus, first and foremost, on making things work. For example, worry about websites and promotional activities after you have released a book, not before. The amount of effort you put in to looking like a business should be proportional to the number of books available to readers.

Remember, your books will be on the market for a very long time so, unlike trade publishers who need to pull in the bulk of their revenue during the three to six months following a book's release, you have the luxury of building your business—especially the part of looking like you're in business—as your actual business grows.

A GOING CONCERN

One of the things that made **Star Wars** (Episode IV) so remarkable when it opened in 1977 was the astonishing degree to which George Lucas's universe, with its scuff marks and exhaust stains, looked lived in. Thanks to a long tradition of using liberal quantities of plastic and chrome in depictions of the World of Tomorrow, prior movies and television programs with futuristic settings favored minimalist, streamlined designs. In contrast to those antiseptic clichés, Luke Skywalker's world was cluttered, dingy, and full of sharp edges and loose ends—much like the world in which we live.

The old aphorism, "If it looks too good to be true, it probably is," applies with a vengeance in the virtual worlds of the Internet. Things that are too bright and shiny, whether it's the enthusiastic salesperson or the glossy brochures for the vacation timeshare they're pressuring you to buy, are always suspect. It's not that older is necessarily better; it's that a business that shows signs of having been around for a while is more likely to be a going concern that will continue to be around after you buy their products or services.

While you will probably have nothing more than an online presence as an artisan publisher, you want your virtual façade to look lived in so that your readers are willing to believe you too are a going concern.

Specifically, your website should look like it serves multiple purposes and is constantly evolving to address new needs. The virtual equivalent of looking lived-in is all the little evidence of sustained attention. Nothing screams amateur like a site thrown together over a weekend that hasn't been updated for more than a year.

An online presence, however, is much more than a single website. While there is no special mix of blogs, profiles, reviews, and social media activity that guarantees success, all of the sites and services you touch as an artisan publisher should be cross-linked and integrated. Setting up and maintaining all of those interrelationships reinforces the sense that you have a going concern.

By this point in our discussion of the artisan way, it should come as no surprise to you that there are no shortcuts. The only way to give your online presence a lived-in feel is by living in it. Like furniture advertisements, which always look staged regardless of the detail the set dressers add, it doesn't take long to recognize a neglected website.

But this is actually good news: an authentic web presence is not a function of clever website design or tricky search engine optimization campaigns; an authentic web presence is a function of an authentic presence on the web over time. That is, if you approach your online façade with the same craftsmanship and integrity that you devote to your artisan publishing readers will recognize that yours is a going concern.

PRICING AND VALUE

Zoe Winters initially priced her e-book novellas at ninety-nine cents because she wanted to build her audience. After a while she decided to increase her prices. Money was part of it: with a 35% royalty it takes a lot of ninety-nine cent e-book to make a living. But it was the attitude of the people buying her inexpensive books that pushed her over the edge. She said:

"... there [are many] readers who buy at 99 cents just to hoard. They don't read, they just buy thinking maybe they'll "get around to it". But they didn't invest enough money in it to really care if they ever read it or not. And many who do read, act "entitled". A strange but true rule of business is that the customers paying the least amount for a product or service always complain the most and try to squeeze more out of you. ... Then there was the fact that I wanted to cultivate a loyal following and most people who expect e-books to be 99 cents aren't that loyal. They're shopping by price as their main deciding factor." [12]

Winter's experience reminded me of the heady days of shareware in the late '80s and early '90s. The pre-Internet world of modems and dial-up bulletin board systems became a remarkably efficient way to distribute software without the costs associated with major software publishers—who were very good at printing catalogs and putting boxes with disks and manuals into stores.

Shareware authors had the same pricing options: undercut to build audience or charge more for value. The interesting thing about software is that higher-priced packages tended to do better because people buying software for their personal computers associated value, quality, and security with the higher price.

Of course, it's not as simple as, "expensive equals good,"

but there is a tendency to treat something that's cheap as … well, cheap.

This is not to say that you should never price your e-book at ninety-nine cents—it might be a market savvy thing to do if it's the first volume in a series—but do you really want people to think that your books aren't worth any more than a three or four minute song?

SUSTAINABILITY

No discussion of pricing and value can ignore the specter of large companies like Walmart and Amazon that seem to be dedicated to destroying their competition through a relentless low-price strategy. Jeff Bezos, Amazon's CEO, has said, "Your margin is my opportunity." The opportunity Amazon's most vocal critics believe Bezos has in mind is to establish a monopoly and then raise prices—the very thing they would do if they were running Amazon. Of all the things critics are willing to believe about Bezos and Amazon, the one thing they refuse to believe is that Amazon is doing exactly what their CEO says they are doing: "There are two kinds of companies: those that work to try to charge more and those that work to charge less. We will be the second."

There are several lessons an artisan publisher should take from Amazon's success to date.

First, Amazon can offer low prices because the entire company is structured not just to survive but to thrive on low profit margins. Like the differing degrees of fuel economy among various models of automobile, other companies that were structured to require higher profit margins simply could not keep up. Similarly, many authors can make a living from books that a traditional publisher would reject because the return on investment wouldn't be large enough to offset their higher costs. And at a personal level, your goal is to structure your expenses and financial obligations so that you can stay in the business of writing and publishing your work even if it only generates a modest profit.

Second, as a company focused on, "work[ing] to charge less," Amazon is really in the business of delivering more value per customer dollar over time. Jeff Bezos said:

> "I very frequently get the question: 'What's going to change in the next 10 years?' ... I almost never get the question: 'What's not going to change in the next 10 years?' And I submit to you that that second question is actually the more important of the two — because you can build a business strategy around the things that are stable in time." [13]

Artisan publishers aiming to practice their craft for the long term need a similar focus on the unchanging elements of their business. People will always value a good story, well told, regardless of the delivery medium. But more than simply focusing on core competencies, artisan publishers need to understand that, like Amazon, they too are in the business of delivering more value to readers over time. Specifically, each subsequent project you publish adds to the value of earlier projects by creating a growing body of work for readers to enjoy. Shakespeare, for example, would have far less cultural significance if he had produced only a handful of plays.

CHAPTER 42.

ARTISAN MARKETING

A deep and pervasive fear all artisan publishers share is that the book into which we've poured so much time, energy, love, and devotion will, upon its release, be met with thunderous silence.

Many of the people giving advice about new opportunities in publishing focus on the problem of discoverability: with millions of books from which to choose, how will you make your book stand out so readers can find it? Their answers cluster around the theme of making as big a splash as possible. The problem with big splashes is that it doesn't take long for others, who have access to exactly the same resources you do, to learn how to make their own big splash. But when everyone is making a big splash, no splash seems big. And soon you're running as fast as you can just to stay in place.

So what can you, as an artisan, do to market your work?

BEING DIFFERENT IN THE SAME WAY

Teenagers instinctively roll their eyes when confronted with the cliché question, "If everyone else jumped off the bridge would you jump too?" As parents, we recognize the futility and potential long-term consequences a young person risks by trying to be different just like all the other young people are trying to be different because we once made the same mistakes. But when you're just starting out and it looks like others in similar circumstances are succeeding by doing certain things it's hard to believe you shouldn't do those things too.

Perhaps that's why many people who decide to forgo working with trade publishers in favor of taking their own projects to market on their own terms try to do the very same thing that the organizations they've chosen not to work with would do to promote their books when they reach the market.

Independent publishing is not just possible but viable because the major trade publishers don't have a monopoly on the best way to reach readers.

This is not to say that all of the old ways of promoting a book—high profile reviews, advertisements, and book tours—are no longer useful but rather that they have been reduced from the tools of choice to simply another option.

Aside from, "Don't offend potential readers," there are no rules defining the right way or the wrong way to market a book. Some approaches seem generally more effective than others, and you would be well advised to pay attention to what has worked for other people, but ultimately the only issue that matters for you as an artisan publisher is what works for your books.

As with everything else about artisan publishing, marketing requires the courage to try and fail and try again.

LAUNCH, RELEASE, AND AVAILABILITY

Scarcity motivates people. If something is available for only a limited time, you must act or lose the opportunity.

Hollywood has mastered the pattern of artificial scarcity. Thanks to a limited number of screens and a limited engagement time, the release of a long anticipated movie is an event that draws a great many people into the theaters.

A few book releases have managed to create the same sort of fervor, with fans lining up in bookstores to be the first to purchase a book when the clock strikes midnight and the store is allowed to begin selling. But most book releases are not so carefully coordinated because most readers don't know the book exists yet. That's why publishers and authors turned to the book launch as a way to jumpstart awareness, demand, and ultimately sales.

A book launch—whether it's a single, splashy event or a multi-city tour—where we stand proudly with our new book, the center of attention of literate friends and strangers, is a big part of the fantasy most of us have about being a published author. Launches are necessary, however, not because it's culturally important to welcome a new book into the world of letters but because new books will generally be on sale for only four to six months.

Electronic publishing frees us from the short-term sales merry-go-round of the business model of commercial publishing. Unfortunately, after celebrating our independence from the old style of publishing, we try to release and launch books the same way they do. A book's performance in the weeks and months following its release no longer predicts its long-term success because e-books are never removed from their online shelves or go out of print. In fact, artisan publishers who don't have the budget to purchase a media blitz in conjunction with creating a release event, find that their books commonly take a year or more to build an audience and begin generating significant sales.

One of the things artisan publishers, particularly those who have some experience with traditional publishing, find challenging is understanding the structural differences between the two lines of business. Many of your expectations and assumptions about how the business of books works are based on a system that depended upon release events and relatively short shelf-life to compel readers to come to the bookstore and purchase books. Now that books can be available indefinitely, you'll get a far better return by making your book enticing to readers instead of trying to compel them to buy it right away.

FREE IS NOT A SILVER BULLET

The prophets of the digital millennium, a utopia of always-on, uber-connected, instant gratification, cry from their virtual street corners that free is the way to attract eyeballs. But with all the talk of boldly going into an infinitive-splitting future, we conveniently overlook the fact that there are hoary institutions—built on the carcasses of dead, ink-smeared trees—that have been providing free content for eons in Internet time. These radical centers of free reading are called libraries. Going to a library isn't as convenient as clicking a link in your browser, but for more than a century it has been possible, if they were willing to put forth a little effort, for readers to sample an author's work for free.

And what have we learned from our centuries-long experience with libraries?

Free doesn't guarantee an audience: yes, you might decide you like an author well enough to go buy their books. But you might also decide you dislike an author so much you are never going to buy his or her books.

When we turn our attention to marketing, there's a subtle pitfall, which has been encouraged by the owners of broadcast media, of confusing an audience with customers: it's not about maximizing eyeballs, it's about maximizing purchases.

An audience is not a tangible commodity. Even with the necessities of life, purchasing a product once is no guarantee that someone will do so again. And when it comes to literature very few authors are so good—or so well promoted—that readers will automatically buy each new book. Publishing something well–received simply increases the likelihood that people will pay attention to you in the future.

Many businesses use a free offer to build a contact list, not an audience. For those businesses it stands to reason that if the customer needed one product they will likely need a related product. You can certainly use a free book to entice readers to sign up for your newsletter, but the argument that if they like one of your books they will like others is more tenuous than the analogous retail argument.

Free works best for artisan publishers when they have more than one book to sell. The difference between introducing readers to your body of published work and getting them to sign up for a newsletter is that they can purchase other books now.

Free is not a magic bullet that will catapult you into bestsellerdom. It is simply one more tool to use if it makes sense to do so. In fact, free is best understood as one end of the pricing spectrum instead of thinking of it as a separate marketing tool. Just like everything else you do as an artisan publisher, free is a tool that you should use with skill and judgment, and not simply because everyone else is doing it.

ADVOCACY FOR ARTISANS

Time and again studies show that the single most important factor in selecting a new book to read is a recommendation from a friend or trusted source. In the context of the rise of the Internet and social media, contemporary wits have updated the time–honored notion of word-of-mouth to be word-of-mouse. Now, instead of tedious one–on–one conversations, you can reach thousands of your closest friends with a few keystrokes and/or clicks. Unfortunately, there's one critical but easily overlooked difference between word–of–mouth and word–of–mouse: a recommendation only works if it comes from a disinterested party.

The new world of frictionless, costless e-publishing doesn't change the need for advocacy. You may be able to establish a reputation by building an online social network, and you may inspire followers to promote your work, but to be credible you need independent readers willing to expend their own time and resources to vouch for your work.

One of the few things you can't do as an artisan

publisher is be your own advocate. Clearly you must put a great deal of time and effort into promoting your work. But no matter how much effort you put into marketing it can never become advocacy because you're not a disinterested party.

If your artisan publishing effort expands to include other authors, you can become an advocate for their work to a small degree. But compared to the major publishing houses, which have the financial wherewithal to lavish seven-figure advances on celebrities, your own investment will hardly stand out.

The practical upshot is that in order to succeed as an artisan publisher you must nurture a network of independent advocates without any of the structural advantages enjoyed by large publishing companies. Moreover, you will have to compete with those companies for readers' attention every step of the way.

Once you've exhausted all the promotional gimmicks, the only sustainable way to build credibility and to attract advocates is to keep showing up: to consistently deliver high quality content. The game you're playing as an artisan publisher—indeed the only game you can play—is a slow, patient one.

BE A TORTOISE

You may have noticed that I haven't provided any marketing checklists. There are no tips, tricks, or techniques in this guide that will ensure the success of your book. It is, in part, a matter of pragmatism: any advice I give you about specific promotional strategies will likely be obsolete by the time you read it. But there is a deeper reason for side-stepping the specifics. Paul St John Mackintosh asked:

"Beyond marketing, nothing builds presence like a good platform, and Amazon has the best. But its omnipresence means that everyone is studying it, learning it, tweaking their offerings and strategies to take advantage of its quirks. Now what if all the self-publishers apply that same knowledge at the same time?" [14]

The answer, according to Syndrome, the villain from **The Incredibles** who planned to sell technology that would give everyone the equivalent of superpowers, is, "And once everyone's super … no one will be." That is, as soon as users learn how to game a system and everyone adopts the tactics, the system returns to an equilibrium where no one has any special advantage.

In the market for books, it's simply not worth the effort to constantly fiddle with pricing and promotions. In the long run you'll earn more from writing another book than from putting the equivalent amount of effort into trying to push the sales of existing book. Each new book tends to improve the sales of previously published books because each new book attracts new readers to your body of work.

As Aesop pointed out so long ago, in races like this, the tortoise actually has the advantage over the hare.

CHAPTER 43.

THE ILLUSION OF A NATIONAL BOOK CULTURE

The single greatest (and most rarely voiced) fear of those considering the path of the artisan publisher is that they will be ignored—or worse, condemned—by the national book culture. Who doesn't want to be the toast of the town, recommended by critics, booksellers, and librarians everywhere? Can one even be a writer if not recognized as such by the keepers of our cultural institutions?

But here's a dirty secret: literary fame is actually a measure of the number of people using you and your work to make money. It has nothing to do with your artistic merit, cultural value, or intrinsic worth and everything to do with how much of other people's commerce you can drive.

The idea that publishers are the source of quality assurance for the literate world is a fascinating part of the construct of a national book culture that serves to obscure the self–interest of all the parties in the commercial bookselling chain.

JAMES PATTERSON'S LAMENT

In 2013, James Patterson placed ads in the **New York Times Book Review** and **Publishers Weekly** asking, "[The federal government] has stepped in to save banks, and the automobile industry, but where are they on the important subject of books?" [15] While many people scoffed at the notion of the government bailing-out commercial publishers, they missed the subtext: Patterson was publically mourning the passing of an idealized (and mostly mythical) national book culture.

Patterson listed thirty-eight *important* books in the ad and asked, "What will happen if there are no more books like these?"

My answer is, "Not much." I've read only four of the thirty-eight books in Patterson's list (though to be fair, I've been affected by a few others—mostly in the form of movies).

To understand my answer, however, you need to know that I belong to the group of people who should care about that list: I was educated at an elite, East-Coast university and hold a post-graduate degree. My home is filled with books—more than a ton the last time we moved. What, then, is wrong with me? Why, in terms of Patterson's list, am I so poorly read?

Because I was reading other things.

There was a time when it mattered what was on television: with only three broadcast networks, you could always find people who had watched what you watched last night and wanted to talk about it. Now with hundreds of cable channels, video on demand services, and YouTube, no one makes any assumptions about what you may have watched.

With the possible exception of the Bible, not only is the same true for books, it's been a very long time since there were few enough books that one could make any assumptions about what most people had read.

So why do we continue to wring our hands over the impending demise of literary culture?

THE CULTURAL SMOKE SCREEN

Through a complex web of bestseller lists, reviewers and critics, English professors, librarians, booksellers, book clubs and so on, trade publishers have attempted to create the commercial equivalent of a required reading list that everyone must go buy—and, by extension, justifying their existence as the uniquely qualified purveyors of our most important cultural expressions. The publishing ecosystem expends a great deal of energy trying to create a sense of urgency by making readers feel they are behind or missing out on the leading edge of literary culture.

Publishers are fundamentally paper distributors that have historically bundled value–added editorial and marketing services. This observation upsets publishing professionals who don't want to see their shared illusion of the grand cultural edifice of publishing reduced to something as prosaic as a retail distribution system.

Grocers don't need to convince us that food is important—we all must eat. Booksellers, who operate the same kind of business (one where they must regularly turn their inventory to keep customers coming back for fresh products), created a cultural imperative because there is nothing else driving us to consume more books.

GATEKEEPING, ADVOCACY, AND PROMOTION

We often talk of the gatekeepers who stand between us and our publishing aspirations. We even say things like, "vetted by publishers"—as if publishers where somehow the guardians of all that is good and true. Unfortunately our sloppy language leads to sloppy thinking about the role of publishers. Specifically, we confuse gatekeeping, advocacy, and promotion.

Gatekeeping means choosing who will pass and who will be excluded. It also implies an endorsement: you know you're one of the cool people if the bouncer at the club lets you past the velvet rope.

Advocacy is an important part of maintaining the social fabric. Obvious self-interest makes us wary of both the promoter and the product. But if a nominally disinterested party champions someone's cause, we take it as evidence that the case has merit. That's why we still need lawyers and agents.

Promotion, of course, is an effort to get people to buy one's products.

Keeping authors separate from publishers creates the illusion of advocacy. The publishing industry has expanded on that illusion by developing layers of structural advocates to mask their promotional activities. From the distribution chain, with its wholesalers, distributors, and retailers, to the web of reviewers, booksellers, librarians, and teachers who promote books and reading in general, the publishing industry, which is as commercial as any other, camouflages itself as a cultural institution.

Gatekeeping and taste-making may once have been the domain of the bookseller when they selected titles to carry from the publishers' catalogs. Now, however, publishers purchase placement in the stores: the stack of books near the entrance has nothing to do with the bookseller's opinion of the book and everything to do with the chain's corporate promotions office's opinion of the publisher's cooperative marketing money.

WHAT ABOUT THE READERS ... AND THE WRITERS?

While it is true that shared references are a cornerstone of culture, the idea that a book's importance is best measured by the number of concurrent readers is one that only benefits trade publishers and booksellers.

In the past, writers had to play the commercial lottery of getting published because it was the only game in town. Unfortunately, that system fostered an all–or–nothing mentality: your book was a failure if it wasn't the talk of the nation.

Rejecting a manuscript because it wasn't sufficiently commercial meant the trade publisher believed the book wouldn't sell in the volume they needed to turn a short-term profit. But that judgment took none of the needs of readers or writers into account.

Tracy Hickman tells writing conference audiences, "It doesn't matter if you're published. Being published is nothing. It is everything to be read."

An author needs readers, but he or she doesn't need every reader. In fact, it is not possible to write one book that will appeal to every single reader. What is possible, thanks to the recent explosion in publishing opportunities, is to write things that will be read because the distance between writer and reader is now much smaller.

* * *

Even though there has never been a single national book culture, Patterson's lament is worth considering:

- What does literary culture mean in the new world of textual abundance created by Amazon and its ilk?
- Who decides which novels belong in the canon of literature with which everyone should be familiar?

The answer is we do.

In the infinite online catalog, we can actually vote (through reviews, for example), for the texts we consider worthwhile. Like democracy, the system isn't perfect, but over time it will tend to work better than tyranny, however benign.

CHAPTER 44.

STRATEGIC PUBLISHING IN AN AGE OF ABUNDANCE

What should you do if you want to stake a claim in the electronic frontier?

In the immortal words of **The Hitchhiker's Guide to the Galaxy**, "Don't panic."

IGNORE BURSTING BUBBLES

One thing that becomes apparent after you've spent some time participating in the modern, hyper-connected world is that there's always a gold rush: there's always a wave to catch or an opportunity to make your fortune by getting in on the ground floor of something.

For publishers of all types and sizes, e-books are the current gold rush. People look at the dramatic triple digit growth of e-book sales early in the digital revolution, compare it with smaller current growth rates, and conclude they have to get involved now or they'll miss out. Of course, what's really going on is that the total sales volume today dwarfs the sales of those years when the growth rate looked so dramatic because the market was growing from nothing to something.

But swelling and bursting opportunity bubbles are irrelevant to artisan publishers because they are playing a long-term game. They understand that over time the daily churn is just noise—what's fashionable this season will be oh-so-tired next. They stay focused on the only goal that matters:

GETTING YOUR DONKEY TO MARKET

Searching the Internet for resources and advice to support your artisan publishing efforts, you're likely to come away believing the only way a modern author can succeed is to be all things to all people. According to common web 2.0 wisdom, if you aren't working every possible social media channel you're missing readers and leaving money on the table. But it's not enough to produce a constant stream of social content that builds your personal brand; you've also got to try to stay ahead of the pack of other self-publishers by jumping on the latest promotional techniques and ranking optimizations to keep your work visible and discoverable.

Aesop tells the fable of the man, the boy and the donkey who were traveling to market. A passerby chides them for not riding the donkey so the man puts the boy on the donkey. Someone else berates the lazy boy for making his father walk so they switch places. They try every combination of riding and walking in response to new complaints until the donkey dies. An old man who watched all of this pronounces the moral, "Please all, and you will please none."

Most writers understand, where storytelling is concerned, that chasing trends is a losing proposition:

long–form fiction takes long enough to produce that by the time you recognize and act on a trend it will be old news. Yet they forget the lesson when they become publishers and chase the latest marketing trends in a vain effort to ensure their success. This approach to business is all the more ironic in the context of literature where the books we remember are the ones that broke new ground and not the ones that delivered more of the same.

So, to what should you pay attention?

The simple answer is you should mind your own business.

A true artisan works confidently. Where managing your business affairs is concerned, working confidently means not being perturbed by the constant turmoil in the market. Follow the example of general Ulysses S. Grant who, when an adjutant reported on Confederate movements during a battle in the U. S. Civil War and fretted about what their enemies were planning, said, "I'm not worried about what the rebel general might do. I'm worried about what I'm going to do."

What, then, should your strategy be as you're minding your own business?

ESTABLISH A FOOTPRINT

If you are an unpublished author, it's easy to feel left out as one metaphorical old coot after another runs into town crying, "There's gold in them e-books! Saddle up your back list and go west!"

You will find the temptation to rush the release of your first manuscript nearly irresistible. Should you give in, you will almost certainly be disappointed by your book's reception—not because people won't notice but because people, with all the other things clamoring for their attention, won't continue to notice.

Insofar as media is concerned, we've moved from an age of scarcity into an age of abundance. Where readers may once have been content to wait for a favorite author's next book, people now expect everything to be available when they find something of interest.

Netflix, the Internet video streaming service, produces original content for their subscribers. Instead of following the half–century–old television industry precedent of releasing a new episode each week to keep viewers coming back, they release the entire series when it's finished. They do that because their subscriber data shows viewers prefer to watch a series all at once. Your readers are similar: they will be much happier if, after finding your book, they can find your other books instead of having to wait while you write.

Beyond gratifying readers, however, each book you release creates another opportunity for people to find one of your books and, through that book, find the rest of your work. Each book, in effect, becomes an advertisement for your other books. You should, of course, take advantage of this opportunity by including a catalog of all your available works in the back of each book. But even if you don't, contemporary Internet users know that a quick search will help them find anything else you may have published.

You can take it one step further by using one or a few of your books as loss–leaders to attract new readers. Back in the dark ages of floppy drives and modems, the old shareware game formula was that you'd give away one free volume to entice users to purchase the other two. Three volumes was the magic number because it created a sufficiently large conceptual footprint (i.e., you received twice as much as you got for free when you bought the game).

Three is a good rule of thumb: you are generally further ahead not releasing any books until you can release at least three. As with shareware, three books create a large conceptual footprint, implying, among other things, that you're a serious writer and it would be worth a reader's while to invest in your work because you will likely produce more.

Like most other *overnight successes*, you'll probably *suddenly* make it in e-books only after you've put in the patient work to build a large-enough footprint.

THE SAVINGS PROBLEM

We all know we should save for our retirement. Thanks to the magic of compound interest, the more money you save early on, the more money you'll earn over the long term. The problem for most of us is that there are far more pressing demands for money when we're starting out so our savings plans remain more theory than reality. The best answer is to save a small amount each and every month. In addition to establishing the habit of savings, this practice allows us to take advantage of dollar cost averaging. [16] Dollar cost averaging means regularly investing a consistent amount without regard to market fluctuations. Over the long run, in a growth market, you'll always come out ahead.

As an artisan publisher, your business model is a lot like the savings problem: the larger your catalog of publications, the more you'll sell. But your catalog is small (or nonexistent) when you're starting out and so your sales during your first few years are likely to be as unimpressive as your savings record during your early twenties. While your sparse catalog may make you anxious and impatient, like dollar cost averaging, your best business strategy as an artisan publisher is to develop and publish titles at a steady, sustainable pace.

* * *

As your patience and resolve are tested, it's important to remember that, in the end, what really matters are the rights you control. Your overall strategic objective is to develop a body of intellectual property that you and your heirs can license or exploit for the full duration of your copyright.

CHAPTER 45.

WHAT SHOULD YOU DO?

So, should you stay, or should you go? As **The Clash** explained in their early 80s punk classic, if you stay there could be trouble, if you go it could be double.

Should you become an artisan publisher? Or would your time be better spent doing something else?

The bad news is that no one knows.

The good news is that no one knows.

DEALING WITH UNCERTAINTY

Faced with uncertainty, many people are paralyzed by fear. If you examine those fears, however, you'll find that what's holding you up is not so much the thing itself but worries about what it might mean: what if you tried something and failed, would others take that as evidence that you are a failure?

There is another, more Zen-like, way to look at uncertainty. We tend to view doubts as the result of moral or intellectual failings. But doubt is only a half-step removed from wonder. As children, our world is full of wonder. We are naturally curious and want to understand why things happen the way they do. One of the side effects of becoming an adult is that our need for security trumps our curiosity. Over time uncertainty comes to be more strongly associated with fear than wonder.

Of course, one should never cast aside hard–won prudence on a whim. Don't walk away from a full-time job because you want to give artisan publishing a whirl. Remember the lessons of your childhood, when trying something meant poking it with a stick, not jumping in feet–first.

Instead of agonizing over what may or may not happen, the best way to confront uncertainty is to give it a try and see what actually happens.

BLOOM WHERE YOU ARE PLANTED

There is an established order to things: movies come out of Hollywood and books come out of New York. The coasts are where the interesting things happen and the middle states are what you fly over. You must go to the established center if you want to succeed. No one will find you if you set up shop off the beaten path.

Except when they do.

Sometimes if you build it, they do come.

Utah boasts a surprising—some would say disproportionate—number of writers and writing conferences. It's hard to say whether the number of writers grew because of the conferences, or the conferences because of the writers, but there is a vibrant, vital writing community in what many would say is the middle of nowhere.

Why?

Because no one there took any notice of the fact that portions of Utah look remarkably like Tatooine or that their western home was far away from the bright center of the publishing universe. Instead, they devoted themselves to what they loved: they wrote and they found like-minded people who wanted to get together periodically and talk about writing. They didn't worry (too much) about what was going on elsewhere or, more importantly, what anyone else thought.

Sometimes the best way to succeed is to forget about the established order, pursue your fascination, and invite others to share what you've discovered.

WHAT IS SUCCESS?

Publishing is becoming ephemeral.

As authors, when everyone was playing the same game we had a basis to compare, compete, and excel. Now everyone is playing a different game—and the playing field keeps moving around. Along with everything else people don't know in the publishing industry, we no longer know what success looks like.

The best investing advice is to establish your own goals, invest for the long term, ignore day-to-day market fluctuations, and exit when you reach your goals. The best artisan publishing advice is similar: establish your own definition of success, work toward that, and don't worry about what anyone else is or isn't doing.

PUTTING IT IN PERSPECTIVE

So what's the moral to this story?

You'll never have the financial wherewithal, the marketing reach, or command the reader attention that major publishers enjoy. With so much stacked against you, should you give up? Should you just hang up your passion along with the other skeletons in your closet of broken dreams?

Take a deep breath and be still.

As consuming as our cares about craft, promotion, and publishing in general are, every so often it is good to step back and put our problems in perspective. There are far too many people who are unable to join us in bemoaning the changes buffeting the culture of letters because they're distracted by trifling annoyances like not starving, succumbing to disease, or becoming a casualty.

Humans have always dreamed and told stories. That we have the time and the means to catch those dreams and render them in an enduring form, which has the potential to touch the lives of far more people than could ever fit around a campfire, is something our ancestors would find miraculous.

For much of human history only the rich and powerful were able to leave a durable legacy because palaces, temples, and monuments of stone were about your only options if you wanted future generations to know you once existed. In time, books provided a more effective way to preserve your thoughts and feelings for those who would follow, but they were still largely the province of an elite sliver of society. Now billions of us can write for the ages.

Of course, nothing is ever certain. A host of calamities, from asteroids to zombies, could reduce us to fossilized traces. But in the grand scheme of things, we're incredibly fortunate to have words to worry about, rejections to receive, and the perpetually perplexing publishing industry to enjoy.

NO ONE KNOWS ANYTHING

Pigeons. Many city-dwellers call them flying rats. The fact that they are ubiquitous enough to earn our contempt is proof of their ecological success. While naturalists can list the biological traits enabling pigeons to thrive in our urban environments, the most important element of their success is social: they watch each other. When the flock descends to its accustomed feeding ground, if some pigeons go somewhere else, others will notice and follow on the chance that the nonconformist birds have found a better food source. The net effect of the pigeon version of keeping up with the Joneses is that collectively the flying rats do a good job of exploiting all the food available in their environment.

William Goldman is generally credited with the observation, "In Hollywood, no one knows anything." It's also true outside of Hollywood, particularly in those dimensions of life involving entertainment or leisure.

Things change.

Nothing is guaranteed.

What works today may not work tomorrow. And the people who think they know what works are likely wrong—if not now, then soon.

Why?

Because people are like pigeons: success attracts imitators. Every modern cliché was once an innovation so fresh and delightful that everyone picked it up and used it until it became ubiquitous enough to earn our contempt.

So, what's the answer?

Like the tortoise, slow and steady wins the race. The hares getting all the attention right now will flash and fizzle. Instead of trying to chase the hares, stay on course and focus on steady progress. Concentrate on producing value the time–tested way: write compelling, well–told stories. Whether they're painted on cave walls, told around campfires, hand–written on papyrus, set with movable type, encoded in magnetic fields and streams of electrons, or beamed directly into readers' brains, people will always want new stories.

And in the end it really doesn't matter what anyone else does. The only relevant question at the final accounting is, "What did you do?" If you can say, like a true artisan, that every day you tried to do your best, they can't ask for a better answer.

ACKNOWLEDGEMENTS

This series of writing guides grew out of a collection of posts on my blog, **The Laws of Making**, representing a conversation of sorts with the following people, each of whom helped me sharpen my thinking about writing and the writing life:

Podcasts: Sarah Eden, Patrick Hester, Marion Jensen, Mary Robinette Kowal, Mur Lafferty, L.E. Modesitt, Brandon Sanderson, Howard Tayler, Dan Wells, Robinson Wells.

Conference Panels and Presentations: John Brown, Jaleta Clegg, James Dashner, Bree Despain, Jessica Day George, Laura Hickman, Tracy Hickman, Jeanette Ingold, Clint Johnson, Lynn Kurland, Scott Livingston, Leslie Muir Lytle, Brandon Mull, Sheila Nelson, Janette Rallison, Sandra Tayler, Joanna Volpe, Stacy Whitman, Julie Wright.

Posts: Brunonia Barry, Holly Black, Livia Blackburn, Michael Bourret, Sarah Callender, Adam Carolla, Toni McGee Causey, Eric Cummings, Julie Danes, Stephanie DeVita, Anne Gallagher, Janet Grant, Elizabeth Gumport, Meghan Cox Gurdon, P.J. Hoover, Austin Kleon, Stina Linderblatt, Annette Lyons, Juliet Marillier, Bob Mayer,

Jael McHenry, Heather Moore, Aprilynne Pike, Simon Pulman, Erin Reel, Holly Root, Kristine Kathryn Rusch, Jon Sternfeld, Rebecca Talley, Heidi M. Thomas, Carrie Vaugh, John Vorhaus, Chuck Wendig, Scott Westerfeld, Zoe Winters, Julie Wright, Howard Yoon, Sara Zarr.

Blogs: Nathan Bransford, Jessica Faust, Rachelle Gardner, Jeff Hirsch, Mary Kole, Kristin Nelson, Kate Testerman, Becca Wilhite.

Thank you.

NOTES

I've provided the following links for those who would like further information about sources of quotes and other selected topics. Some of the links go to Amazon because there are no better sources of information. I've included those links for your convenience. They are not affiliate links and I receive no benefit if you make a purchase.

NOTES FOR SURVIVING THE WRITING LIFE

CHAPTER 3: THE WORLD OF COMMERCIAL WRITING

[1] Janet Grant, an agent with **Books and Such Literary Agency** posted her comments on covers and trailers turning book releases into old news on her agency blog in January 2011. See: http://www.booksandsuch.biz/blog/stuff-you-need-to-know-for-2011-hold-back-those-book-trailers-and-book-covers/

[2] Agent Rachelle Gardner made her comments about the pace at which the publishing industry moves on her blog in June 2011. See: http://www.rachellegardner.com/2011/06/why-is-publishing-so-slow/

CHAPTER 4: YOUR ROLE AS A COMMERCIAL WRITER

[3] The study of fairness in brown capuchin monkeys was published in 2003 and reported in several places including **National Geographic News**: http://news.nationalgeographic.com/news/2003/09/0917_030917_monkeyfairness.html

CHAPTER 5: WRITING ADVICE

[4] Annette Lyons shared her characterization of writers as storytellers or wordsmiths on the **Writing on the Wall** blog in March 2011. See: http://writingonthewallblog.blogspot.com/2011/03/2-sides-of-good-writer.html

[5] Holly Root advised writers not to over-think their queries on the **Waxman Agency** blog in November 2009. See: http://waxmanagency.wordpress.com/2009/11/06/with-a-boulder-of-salt/

[6] Nathan Bransford advised writers to sweat the query details on his blog on the same day in November 2009. See: http://blog.nathanbransford.com/2009/11/get-big-stuff-right.html

CHAPTER 6: SURVIVING THE WRITING LIFE

[7] Chuck Wendig explored reasons to stop writing on his **Terrible Minds** blog in June 2011. See: http://terribleminds.com/ramble/2011/06/08/six-signs-its-high-time-to-give-up-writing/

Walt Whitman sounded his barbaric yawp in "Song of Myself" from **Leaves of Grass**. See line 1333 at [8] "Representative Poetry Online:" http://rpo.library.utoronto.ca/poem/2288.html

[9] Agent Howard Yoon shared his advice to take rejections personally on the **Guide to Literary Agents** blog at Writer's Digest in May 2011. See: http://www.writersdigest.com/editor-blogs/guide-to-literary-agents/agent-advice-howard-yoon-of-ross-yoon-literary

[10] Author Natalie Whipple discussed patience while her manuscript was on submission with her agent on her blog in a December 2010 post that is well worth your time to read in its entirety. See: http://betweenfactandfiction.blogspot.com/2010/12/what-ive-learned-from-being-on.html

CHAPTER 7: YOUR JOB AS A WRITER

[11] Sarah Callender talked about over-confidence, under-confidence, and calling ourselves writers at **Write it Sideways** in November 2011. http://writeitsideways.com/can-you-really-call-yourself-a-writer/

[12] Nathan Bransford provided his ten commandments for happy writers on his blog in March 2009. See: http://nathanbransford.blogspot.com/2009/03/ten-commandments-for-happy-writer.html

CHAPTER 8: GOOD WRITING

[13] Lynne Truss, "That'll do, comma," Eats, Shoots & Leaves, London: Profile Books. 2003. ISBN 1-86197-612-7

NOTES FOR PROFESSIONAL RELATIONSHIPS

CHAPTER 1: IT'S NOT ABOUT YOU

[1] Wikipedia has a good overview of Dale Carnegie's, **How to Win Friends and Influence People**. See: http://en.wikipedia.org/wiki/How_to_Win_Friends_and_Influence_People

CHAPTER 2: DON'T CRITICIZE, CONDEMN, OR COMPLAIN

[2] Jonathan Lethem discussed the importance of focusing on your own game in terms of golf. See: http://leaguewriters.blogspot.com/2010/10/writing-wisdom-of-ages.html

CHAPTER 3: GIVE HONEST AND SINCERE APPRECIATION

[3] Doug Eboch shared the best networking advice ever—to network laterally—on his blog. See: http://letsschmooze.blogspot.com/2008/11/how-not-to-network.html

[4] In a follow-up post, Eboch offered a number of good suggestions for how to go about networking. See: http://letsschmooze.blogspot.com/2008/12/how-to-network.html

CHAPTER 4: AROUSE IN THE OTHER PERSON AN EAGER WANT

[5] Aprilynne Pike discussed the importance of not just getting published but of getting published with the right partners and in the right way in a 2009 post on her blog.

See: http://apparentlyaprilynne.blogspot.com/2009/10/firsts.html

CHAPTER 5: AGENTS

[6] Wikipedia has a nice article on Leprechauns. See: http://en.wikipedia.org/wiki/Leprechaun

[7] At the end of 2010, agents Kate Testerman and Kristin Nelson shared their query stats for 2010. Testerman signed one client out of 4987 queries. Nelson estimates her agency received about 36,000 queries, from which they signed nine new clients.

See Testerman's report at: http://ktliterary.com/2010/12/a-year-in-queries/

See Nelson's report at: http://pubrants.blogspot.com/2010/12/year-in-statistics-2010.html

CHAPTER 7: AUDIENCE

[8] Martin Amis is quoted in a 2011 article in the **Guardian**. See: http://www.guardian.co.uk/books/2011/feb/11/martin-amis-brain-injury-write-children

CHAPTER 9: MARKETING AND PROMOTION

[9] Kevin Smokler discussed his ideas about promotion in an interview at http://wegrowmedia.com/how-to-successfully-promote-your-book-the-kevin-smokler-interview/

CHAPTER 10: AUTHENTIC WEB PRESENCE

[10] Livia Blackburn discussed the effectiveness of author blogs in a 2011 post on her blog. See: http://blog.liviablackburne.com/2011/07/author-blogging-youre-doing-it-wrong.html

[11] Wikipedia has a good overview of the Gartner Hype Cycle. See: http://en.wikipedia.org/wiki/Hype_cycle. The Gartner Hype Cycle diagram is by Jeremykemp at en.wikipedia

NOTES FOR SUSTAINABLE CREATIVITY

CHAPTER 1: THE SUBSTANCE OF ART

[1] See the Wikipedia article on psychological flow. See: http://en.wikipedia.org/wiki/Flow_(psychology)

[2] See the Wikipedia article on the psychological concept of mindfulness. See: http://en.wikipedia.org/wiki/Mindfulness_(psychology)

CHAPTER 4: THE ART OF COLLECTING IDEAS

[3] A Sample of Name Generators on the Internet:

- BehindTheName.com is a site for the, "etymology and history of first names." It has a generator that can be restricted to particular ethnic groups. See: http://www.behindthename.com/random/

- There's a US Census-based name generator at http://www.kleimo.com/random/name.cfm

- Seventh Sanctum™ has a cornucopia of fantasy/gaming-inspired name generators for everything from people to pirate ships. See: http://www.seventhsanctum.com/index-name.php

[4] The description of the study about switching problem-solving styles appeared in a 2011 article on **PsyBlog**. See: http://www.spring.org.uk/2011/05/unusual-thinking-styles-increase-creativity.php

[5] John Lasseter's comments about good ideas were shared in a 2010 post on the **Scribble Junkies** blog. See:

http://scribblejunkies.blogspot.com/2010/12/
animation-101-7-creative-principles-of.html

CHAPTER 5: THE SCIENCE OF USING IDEAS

[6] See Wikipedia for more on James Burke's PBS series called **Connections**: http://en.wikipedia.org/wiki/ Connections_(TV_series)

[7] See Wikipedia for more on Thomas Kuhn's **The Structure of Scientific Revolutions**: http://en.wikipedia.org/wiki/ The_Structure_of_Scientific_Revolutions

CHAPTER 6: THE CREATIVE LIFE

[8] Austin Kleon has expanded his work into a book, called **Steal Like an Artist: 10 Things Nobody Told You About Being Creative**. You can get it at Amazon, Barnes & Noble, IndieBound, and a number of other places. It's well worth your while.

CHAPTER 7: CREATIVE DISCIPLINE

[9] I learned about little systems from Jim McCarthy's **Dynamics of Software Development**. You can learn more about the 1995 edition of the book at Amazon.

NOTES FOR ARTISAN PUBLISHING

CHAPTER 1: ARTISAN PUBLISHING

[1] Agent Jessica Regel shared her thoughts on changes in the publishing industry in an interview posted on the **Guide to Literary Agents** blog: http://www.writersdigest.com/editor-blogs/guide-to-literary-agents/literary-agent-jessica-regel-of-jean-v-naggar-literary-seeks-new-clients

[2] See http://en.wikipedia.org/wiki/The_Innovator%27s_Dilemma for an overview of **The Innovator's Dilemma,** by Clayton Christensen.

[3] Elizabeth Gumport argued that recent is not a synonym for relevant on the **N+1** blog. See: http://nplusonemag.com/against-reviews

CHAPTER 2: A CLEAR VIEW OF THE PUBLISHING INDUSTRY

[4] For more on Mark Twain's book subscription program see: http://rmc.library.cornell.edu/twain/exhibition/subscription/index.html

[5] Learn about Charles Dicken's publishing efforts at: http://www.pbs.org/wnet/dickens/life_publication.html

[6] Kristine Kathryn Rusch explains what publishers really think of writers in a February 2013 post on her blog. See: http://kriswrites.com/2013/02/28/the-business-rusch-the-death-of-publishing

CHAPTER 3: WHY YOU SHOULDN'T CHOOSE ARTISAN PUBLISHING

[7] Keith Cronin, in an article on **Writer Unboxed**, shared the story of his mother reminding him that no one asked

him to be in a band. See: http://writerunboxed.com/2013/05/14/sht-my-mom-said/

[8] Read Robert Frost's, "The Road Not Taken," at http://www.poetryfoundation.org/poem/173536

CHAPTER 4: THE ADVANTAGES OF ARTISAN PUBLISHING

[9] Yuvi Zalkow, in an article on **Writer Unboxed**, explained how liberating the thought of being able to quit can be. See: http://writerunboxed.com/2013/09/29/how-much-wandering-before-im-no-longer-lost/

CHAPTER 5: EDITORIAL CONTROL

[10] You could to much worse that starting your study of editing with Brown and King, **Self-editing for Fiction Writers**. See: Amazon

CHAPTER 6: THE CHALLENGES OF ARTISAN PUBLISHING

[11] Robert M. Sapolsky, "Super Humanity," **Scientific American**, September 2012.

CHAPTER 9: THE ARTISAN PHILOSOPHY OF BUSINESS

[12] Zoe Winters discussed her experience with e-book pricing with Jennifer Mattern on the **All Indie Publishing** blog. See: http://allindiewriters.com/zoe-winters-on-ebook-pricing/

[13] Jeff Bezos in quoted in an interview on The Motley Fool. See: http://www.fool.com/investing/general/2013/09/09/the-25-smartest-things-jeff-bezos-has-ever-said.aspx

CHAPTER 10: ARTISAN MARKETING

[14] Paul St John Mackintosh, on **TeleReads**, speculated about diminishing returns for self-publishing. See: http://www.teleread.com/self-publishing/diminishing-returns-dawn-for-self-publishing/

CHAPTER 11: THE ILLUSION OF A NATIONAL BOOK CULTURE

[15] There were a number of articles about James Patterson's book industry bailout ad. See, for example: http://www.salon.com/2013/04/24/ james_patterson_speaks_out_about_his_ aggressive_book_industry_bailout_ads/

CHAPTER 12: STRATEGIC PUBLISHING IN AN AGE OF ABUNDANCE

[16] For a more comprehensive discussion of dollar cost averaging, see: http://en.wikipedia.org/wiki/ Dollar_cost_averaging